Movable Architecture

Edited by Ross Gilbert

images Publishing

Contents

Foreword / 004

Chapter 01 Usages of Container Buildings / 013
Chapter 02 The Adaptive Design Combinations / 015
Chapter 03 Basic Modification Procedures for
Container Building Construction / 033

Case Studies
Cultural Design
Devil's Corner / 040
Dunraven Container Sports Hall / 046
Zhao Hua Xi Shi Living Museum / 050
KontenerART 2012 / 056
APAP OPEN SCHOOL / 060
Hai d3 / 066
Seoul Youth Zone / 070
Taitung Aboriginal Galleria / 074
OceanScope / 078
Nomadic Museum / 084
Jazzboksen 2016 / 088
Marche in the Forest / 092
Conteneur Bell / 096
So Table Kobe0330 / 100

Commercial Space Design

ContainHotel / 104

Container Stack Pavilion / 110

Ccasa Hostel / 116

Vehicle Charging Station / 124

Alphaville Store / 128

Estoril Praia Clube / 134

CRE-Box / 140

Wisdom Bay / 144

Pop Brixton / 150

UNIT Cafe / 154

THE KRANE / 158

Nike Unlimited Rio / 164

MaxHaus Paulista / 168

HATAGOYA EBISU HOTEL / 172

Bonaire Street Market / 176

Residential Design

Zhengda Colorful City Container Residence Design / 180

Plugin Tower / 188

Módulos habitacionales temporales / 192

Container Casulo / 198

The WFH House / 202

Urban Rigger / 208

Pocket House / 214

Un Dernier Voyage / 218

Cliff House / 224

Nemo House / 230

Office Design

Studio for Two / 234

UNIONKUL STACK II / 238

CONTAINER SALE OFFICE / 246

Bee+ / 252

TIDAL CON-TAINER OFFICE / 256

Innovation Studios / 260

Joshua Tree / 264

Index / 268

Foreword by Ross Gilbert

The Emergence of Container Architecture

As predicted in *Modern Container Architecture*, the release of more containers into ports has helped to inspire a huge wave of new and exciting designs and developments in recent years, with many of the latest and most innovative creative outputs explored here in *Movable Architecture*.

A further source of disruption?

Malcolm P. McLean had a simple yet innovative idea that changed our world.

His innovation wholly disrupted an industry that had no interest in change. Could it be that the very same product could spawn a further disruptive force and drive a revolution in the construction industry?

There are many similarities between the shipping and construction industries. As Aidan Hart outlines in the first book, *Modern Container Architecture* regarding shipping,

"This time consuming and labor-intensive process (break-bulk cargo) was exacerbated by transport delays: ships and carriers would make multiple stops to off-load or pick-up goods along the way."

Simply replace the word "transport" with "weather" and the words "ships and carriers" with "contractors" and the sentence reads:

"This time consuming and labor-intensive process (bricks and mortar construction) was exacerbated by weather delays: contractors would make multiple stops to off-load or pick up goods along the way."

Could McLean's humble steel box disrupt an industry for a second time?

Almost immediately, innovators of the time saw the potential of the shipping container as a building block. On 12 October 1962 Christopher Betjemann, of Lambertville, New Jersey, USA filed four patent claims for a "mobile trade fair"; converting the container into a single transportable building.

In Malmö, Sweden, Fritz Langerbeck filed four patent claims for a 'pop-up' industrial building housed wholly within a shipping container providing one of the earliest modern examples of this nomadic concept.

In 1986, in France, Claude Baudot of Thionville and Vincent Contini of Konacker were busy developing a patent claim for a pre-fabricated modular structure of simple stackable component assembly based on standard container dimensions to allow for easy transport.

Meanwhile in Miami, Florida, on November 23rd,1987, Philip C. Clarke filed the first patent application to physically convert a shipping container into a space suitable for human habitation. Containers were stacked or placed side by side and joined together with a roof, windows, and foundations to provide a habitable building. With a patent granted on August 8th, 1989, the early groundwork had been laid for the adaptation of shipping containers and the future of container architecture.

In the first edition of *Modern Container Architecture*, Hart talked about the advent of containerization and provided case studies that demonstrated the strength, durability, and convenience of using containers. It is clear from the examples illustrated within this book that the container is fast emerging as the preferred basic building block among the key players in today's dynamic global economy in designing and developing appropriate solutions in response to the insatiable demand for various types of accommodation. With their own interpretation of the central ideas generated by Archigram, Kurokawa and Le Corbusier – capsules, pre-fabrication, clip-on and plug-in architecture – more and more developers are increasingly exploring the value in container-based buildings.

Leading designers, provided with a Meccano kit of parts centered around a robust structurally secure building block; the shipping container, are increasingly producing architectural concepts that meet client briefs in terms of budget, form, and function.

Estoril Praia Clube

Why the increase?

The shipping container is the technology of our time. It helped kick-start globalization and the global transport network in the mid-twentieth century, and with changing patterns of trade over the decades, a surplus of stock began to accumulate. This, in turn, paved the way for creativity as innovators began to think about different ways that these structures could be put to better use.

Geopolitical, macroeconomic, demographic, technological, and environmental changes are also key factors here, with volatility and uncertainty becoming the new norm for the operating environment of our planet and our industries. The world cannot stand still. We must work through the uncertainty. As always, one of the key fundamentals for human societal development is shelter – having a roof over our heads.

We are also living in an increasingly urbanized world:

In 1930 – 30% of the world population was living in an urban environment. In 2014 that figure had increased to 54%. And by 2050 it is expected that 66% of the population, an estimated 6 billion people, will be living in urban society.

During this time of unprecedented population growth, increased consumption and pressure on resources, coupled with the effects of climate change and political turmoil; under-investment in the urban environment and economic consolidation threatens to polarize society even further.

As governments worldwide struggle to cope, one grand construction project after the another continues to suffer because of the industry trend of delay after delay and colossal budget over run. Increasingly, there exists the opportunity for bottom-up, organic development on a more human scale.

As the construction industry continues to suffer from productivity woes, and with the decentralization of energy generation and food production continuing to increase a sense of community empowerment is building momentum. Shipping Container Architecture as a low cost, low barrier to entry form of construction has a role to play as the world continues to urbanize and crave affordable accommodation.

So can a commoditized product designed to transport cargo around the globe really emerge, fulfill this demand and disrupt an industry?

While it is important that we do not get too carried away, as perceptions are exceptionally slow to change in the construction industry, there is a true swell towards the re-use of shipping containers. If this is to continue to grow, it is important to understand the dynamics of the shipping container market (both new and used) and how they might impact this growing construction niche.

Figure 1

Iron Ore and Steel Price $/ton

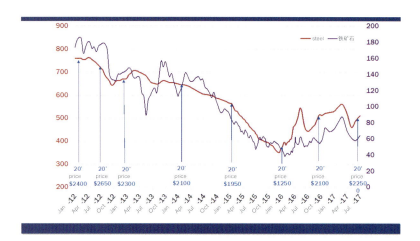

Figure 1: Iron Ore & Steel Price (Source: Container Traders & Innovators Association)

Market Statistics

Commodity Price and Volume

Containers are made predominately from CorTen steel. The overriding steel market commodity prices have an impact on the cost of new containers. As Figure 1 illustrates, the price of steel closely tracks its raw material iron ore. This impacts the market sale price of the new shipping container.

And as illustrated in Figure 2, prices in the second-hand shipping container market broadly follow those of the new build market. Therefore, there is a broad correlation between the price of the raw material and the outturn price.

Consequently, if populations continue to expand and the true implications of a planet with finite limits and resources is understood, there is the potential that the price of a container could face a significant increase should the global demand for steel increase.

Innovations in the sustainability of the product and a switch to water-based paints

Figure 2 provides insight into the dynamic market of shipping container trading. Statistics are collected for Twenty-Foot Equivalent Units (TEUs). Pricing is in US dollars. Therefore, if you are constructing your project in a currency other than US dollars, for example, currency fluctuation is a risk that might not be on your typical construction project register and is one to consider.

Figure 2

New / Used Price Trend

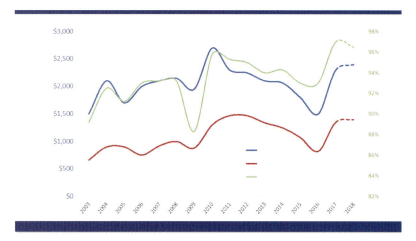

Figure 2: Pricing Trend of New & Used Shipping Containers (Container Traders and Innovators Association)

Figure 3

Sales-TEU

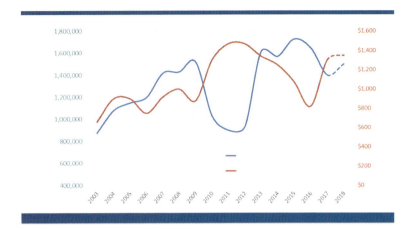

Figure 3: Global TEU Sales Volume & Price (Container Traders & Innovators Association)

There is a clear correlation between the cost of newly built shipping containers and the cost of used or second-hand shipping containers. The data illustrates the newly built market to be more volatile than the second-hand market, which offers more stability.

Figure 3 illustrates a potential elasticity of the container market with prices increasing with a decrease in supply.

Container Market Projections

As Figure 4 illustrates, the global financial crisis had a big impact on the production of shipping containers. This is not surprising as the shipping container is the largest single symbol of globalization. Projections are that as the shipping lines are now starting to replace retiring shipping containers, a higher production demand for 2018/2019 is anticipated, according to the Container Traders and Innovators Association (CTIA).

The nominal capacity of 5 million TEUs is likely to decrease a little to around 4.5 million TEUs production capacity per annum. However, delivery of such volume would require an increase in the labor supply together with significant capital investment in paint drying facilities. Realistically, estimations from the CTIA show that actual production is unlikely to rise above 3.5million TEUs in the short to medium term, as illustrated in Figure 4.

In terms of current volume, the CTIA estimates there are an estimated 38 million TEUs in circulation. Thus, with current production numbers at around 10% of total capacity, the production of new shipping containers remains a relevant factor in determining the price.

Figure 4

Container New Production-TEU

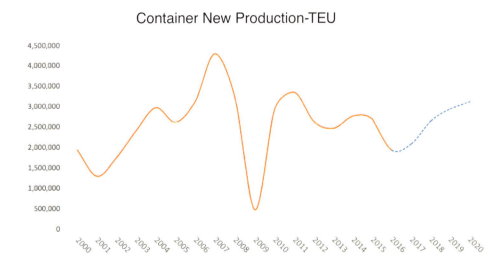

Figure 4: Shipping Container Production in TEU (Source: CTIA)

Types of Shipping Container

There is a wide range of shipping containers in use. Many people are aware of the sizes that containers come in – the majority are 20 feet (6 meters) or 40 feet (12 meter) long, 8 feet (2.4 meters) wide and 8 foot 6 inches (2.6 meters) high.

However, there is an increasing number of 10-foot (3-meter) long containers as well as 45-foot (13.7-meter) long containers. Additionally, there are also hi-cube variants, which are 9 foot 6 inches high rather than the standard 8 foot 6 inches.

Less widely known is the diversity of containers available. The majority of containers in circulation are known as dry vans, the basic type of shipping container. However, there are a number of other types, which can provide the inspiration for further innovations. For example:

(1) Tunnel containers, which have doors on both ends of the container, and which Caboose & Co have successfully adapted to provide CSC-plated nomadic worker accommodation.

(2) Reefer containers, which are insulated by design and incorporate air conditioning equipment to provide a refrigerated transport option. This shipping container, which has straight rather than trapezoidal walls, may, subject to local building codes, be sufficiently insulated for use.

(3) Side-load containers, which have elongated shipping container barn doors on the longer side.

(4) Tank containers, which have an external container frame with a tank integrated into the structure – used for transporting liquids.

(5) Bulk containers (also known as Bulkers) are similar to twenty feet similar to dry vans with hatches included for easy packing and removal of commodities.

(6) Cellular pallet-wide containers, which are specifically designed to transport palletized products 7.9 feet (2.4 meters) in width rather than the standard eight feet (2.438 meters).

In conclusion, it is fair to say that the shipping container is here to stay. It is anticipated that container supply and prices will be maintained in the short to medium term, meaning that global trade will continue to accumulate surplus net supplies in importing countries. From a developer's perspective, this means that container architecture as a design solution and construction methodology has some way to go before it faces any shortage of supply. One of the key factors is to remember is that the trade of shipping containers is a dynamic market influenced by global forces such as financial markets, foreign exchange, and commodity prices.

Applications for Container development

History and Trends

Container architecture is not a recent phenomenon, with a number of examples of buildings constructed from containers prior to Philip Clarke's patent. Buildings have featured a range of shipping container applications, from moveable pop-up offerings, permanent new builds, small to large extensions, to solely structural elements as well as elements that plug into a central infrastructure core.

The development of container architecture follows an interesting path. Its origins are in functional storage, industrial buildings, and simple portable site offices and shelters. The development has evolved and seen pop-up vessels of entertainment, such as Christopher Betjamann's "mobile trade fair" of 1965, the Espresso Coffee Bar featured in *Modern Container Architecture*.

Today, shipping container architecture is being used not just as an affordable build methodology but increasingly as a tool for regeneration – be it as a catalyst for re-building a place after a natural disaster (Re-Start in Christchurch, New Zealand); as a response to excessive demand for a specific need and time-based period (student housing in Keetwonen, Amsterdam, Netherlands); as an affordable temporary accommodation solution (Marston Court, London, UK) or as a method to unlock a development site by decanting, such as the market storage project (Venables Street, London, UK). This evolution from simple construction providing affordable space to a tool for regeneration is an exciting dawn of a new era for container architecture.

Indeed, such is the popularity, functionality, and excitement around container architecture that the offsite construction industry is starting to see increased evidence of purpose-built accommodation containers or building containers for use in specific market sectors, such as hotels, housing, and offices. Companies such as CargoTek UK, Meka USA, and CIMC China to name but a few, have entered this arena.

Considerations when building with containers

Building with containers has a number of advantages. As a building block, they are exceptionally durable and strong. Made from CorTen steel (which rusts to protect itself), the humble container is designed for a nomadic life (10-12 years) in a harsh marine environment. Therefore, placing a container in a fixed location with improved shelter than the open ocean may extend the lifespan significantly. Shipping containers are designed to be stacked one on top of the other, with the bottom shipping container beneath a stack of nine fully laden containers, able to sustain approximately 240 tons above it. It is this strength, when dealing with the relative low loadings of a building and wind, that excites architects as they can cantilever structures out and over each other (Container stack II), invert them (Devils Corner, Hai D3), organized them to sit at juxtaposed angles (Urban Rigger) or tilt them at angles (APAP Open School).

It is this inherent strength that also provides a flexibility, which allows an ease-of-use as a stand-alone or for multiple installations. This strength also enables simple integration with the structural elements required for human circulation and access: stairs, balconies, walkways and roof terraces. The container's strength enables it to offer structural support for these elements and a simpler integration than stand-alone structures would provide.

The availability of containers, across the globe, together with the existing global transport infrastructure, means that large quantities of containers can be assembled in any one place in a relatively short timeframe. One key strength of the container as a building block for a developer or investor is that if there are any delays between construction, deconstruction, or re-use of containers, there is a global network of container infrastructure that can enable simple and cost-effective storage of moveable container buildings.

In addition to their strength, durability, and availability, the re-use of containers in construction is part of an upcycle revolution— re-using an existing product to create new products of greater social, environmental and financial value. As mentioned in *Modern Container Architecture*, one possible reason containers are so prevalent is that the cost of energy needed to melt down and recycle the steel is greater than the eventual scrap material market value.

The Taitung Aboriginal Galleria in Taiwan is a great example of shipping container up-cycling. With over 10,000 containers hauled from the waterways surrounding Taiwan every year, it makes sense to explore creative ways to re-use them.

The sustainability of container architecture does not just stop with the building block though. As evidenced within this book, there are concrete examples of the integration of existing renewable technologies and materials within containers, utilizing things such as rainwater harvesting (Taitung Aboriginal Galleria), natural ventilation (Estoril Praia Clube), photovoltaic panels, hemp, reed, timber, (Zhao Hua Xi Shi Living Museum) and hydroelectric power.

Experimental technologies are also being explored, such as the parametrical roof design in Estoril, which also makes use of the structure's shadows for shading and cooling, and the Cliff House, which is built 100% off-grid.

Furthermore, shipping container architecture is part of, although not exclusively, the offsite construction revolution (a number of projects are still built on site). Globally, embracing reform in the construction industry and adopting a manufactured systems approach to our buildings is a sure-fire way to ensure supply keeps up with demand and that the overall productivity of the industry is improved. There is certainly an urgent need for modernization within the industry to improve and attract the young talent the industry needs to take it forward.

Container architecture can do this for two reasons: firstly it is different, interesting and disruptive; and young people are generally more predisposed to challenge the status quo. Secondly, it can drive the agenda for change. While views are polarized, there is no doubt that the perceptions in construction are slow to change, container architecture generates a lot of interest and increasingly container buildings are designed as a kit of interchangeable objects that are available off-the-shelf. For designers, having this catalog of products to play with, as this publication shows, inspires a unique style of creativity and innovation.

For designers, there are a number of important factors to consider when building with containers. The first thing to remember is that containers were not originally designed for human habitation so careful design work is required to ensure that containers can become suitable living and working spaces. The operational history of each individual container is essential knowledge to have and should be given careful consideration. For example, modern-day dry vans have water-based paint and plastic, bamboo or steel floors, whereas older containers may have tropical hardwood floors that have been treated with pesticides. Details of any chemical treatment are stated on the CSC plate of all containers and these should be considered extremely carefully before beginning any project. A common solution employed for this type of issue is to apply a low VOC industry-compliant epoxy resin, which provides a secure seal against off-gassing. Alternatively, floors can simply be removed and replaced.

The key thing before embarking on any project using shipping containers is to nail the client brief. There are a number of volumetric building blocks available and using a shipping container should not necessarily be the default. The main strength of the shipping container is its ease of transportation, meaning that it can be constructed, deconstructed and re-used elsewhere often at significantly low cost than other volumetric modular alternatives. It is this strength, from a property development perspective, that makes the container the ubiquitous component of temporary meanwhile projects.

Development Trends of Container Architecture

Permanent structures

Estoril Praia Clube features five containers grafted on or clipped into an existing structure to meet the requirement of additional office space. The parametrical roof and use of shadows for shading, energy-efficient natural ventilation, and use of color provide a uniquely striking, functional and ecological extension to the existing football stadium.

Devil's Corner features a similar extension to an existing structure with further demonstration of the use of angles and sustainable materials to create a striking extension to the vineyard in Australia. This is an excellent example of the benefits of using offsite construction to deliver a project in a remote location. Constructing offsite significantly reduces the disruption to the natural environment with the building being transported to site in a completed state for installation and plugging in.

The Living Museum, Zhao Hua Xi Shi, China demonstrates the integration of offsite construction techniques with locally sourced ecological materials such as hemp, reed, and timber. This cultural resort at the foot of the Great Wall of China illustrates how shipping containers can be used effectively in rural settings.

Increasingly, shipping container architecture integrates with both renewable technologies and alternative construction methods. The Cliff House in South Africa is an excellent example of the shipping container being a preferred object of design, with cantilevered container structures integrated with a light gauge cold rolled steel framing system. This is then overlaid and finished with recycled cork flooring, solar photovoltaic panels, a borehole and natural ventilation – resulting in a beautiful off-grid home.

It is encouraging to see this re-use of the container in architectural solutions together with the integration of other renewable technologies and materials. This trend fosters a culture of frugality and an acceptance that we are living on a planet with finite limits. It is essential that developers and designers continue to promote the use and re-use of the resources available to provide beautiful and appropriate architectural creations in the future.

Temporary structures

While there is a role for the shipping container in permanent buildings, it is in the temporary and transient space that container architecture excels. They were first established, as explained in *Modern Container Architecture*, as a solution for pop-ups and in situations of disaster relief. However, the true potential of the shipping container lies in using it as a strategic tool and a catalyst for urban regeneration.

Disaster Relief

As outlined in *Modern Container Architecture*, "Governments, aid agencies, and designers around the world have been opting the use of containers to create accommodation alternatives in the wake of natural disasters... also offering opportunities to deliver critical services in areas with inadequate or failed infrastructure in developing countries."

Pop-up Architecture

Pop-up architecture often features the shipping container as the building block of choice, with spaces created for events, brand activations and entertainment venues that make a statement. Think of the ZU FLUX Adidas Gallery, which leaves "presence without a permanent place" – the strength and transportability of the single container allows it to stand out from the competition.

Interim Use

Projects featured in *Movable Architecture* illustrate an increase in the sophistication of shipping container buildings and their temporary use. Graduating from forms of entertainment to genuine strategic moves in a wider regeneration strategy.

The fast-growing Shanxi province is home to the Container Stack Pavilion Project. The scheme uses the strength and flexibility of the container to cantilever the structures to provide an open plan office and showroom. The structure, painted with a bold, yet simple color scheme, is fully moveable. Once the use of this project has expired, the building will be deconstructed and transported somewhere else for future use.

The HaiD3 project in Dubai is a further example of a demountable moveable building created with shipping containers. The project, which provides incubator space for local creative is an example of using container architecture to kick-start the regeneration of a wider area. This ensures that people and place can begin from day one rather than having to wait for slow and antisocial 'traditional' construction projects to complete before any sense of community can be established.

The floating Urban Rigger project in Denmark takes the concept of interim development a stage further by creating its place (on water) for deployment. This wholly transient structure was devised in response to acute demand for student housing.

These three projects outline some of the key trends in the deployment of temporary shipping container architecture. The container itself is left as untouched as is possible to enable easy transportation and re-use. Roofs are modular and removable where installed. The aesthetic is achieved through color, clip-on facades, and the use of natural materials around the shipping containers rather than traditional cladding solutions. Despite the supposed temporary nature of these projects, the trend to use renewable energies and materials continues with solar PV, hydroelectric, and heat pumps, becoming common features.

The advantage of these approaches from a development perspective is that projects all lend themselves to being deconstructed with ease and speed. They can be easily stored if there is a delay between deployments and they can either be combined or split in future projects and due to the modular nature of their designs may find alternative forms.

In addition to the very projects themselves being adaptive; capable of expanding, contracting or exchanging in response to fluctuating conditions such as climate change or accommodation demand, changeable dwellings can also inspire owners to better express themselves. They engender a more dynamic environment and suggest that a trial and error approach and experimentation is significantly more feasible than previous architectural design systems. The end result is that architectural responses better correspond to patterns of human behavior and relate more to the form of living being sought today.

The container, which is really the technology of our time, has the potential to encourage discord and disruption. The Plugin Tower project from the People's Architecture Office in China is a perfect example of this. The project, which provides affordable housing, is ideal for city infill. The disruptive potential of this temporary or undefined project is significant: it does not require an underground foundation and it circumvents existing strict planning policy requirements for private houses. Capable of being installed by a couple of unskilled workers, this solution can flip the traditionally conservative real estate and construction markets on their heads, particularly for those with lower incomes. The practical concept of store-bought homes emboldens the potential of revolt against the traditional top-down development and regeneration models.

Impact

Compliance & Policy

Globally, the construction industry is slow and resistant to change. Governmental policy and the legislative process move at a glacial pace. The advent of container architecture and what it enables (think plug-in architecture) has the potential to be extremely disruptive, to challenge ways of thinking, and to change the status quo.

Looking again at the Plugin Tower example, this project is not just breaking the rules; it is inventing a new game that could potentially trigger a metamorphosis in the built environment as we know it.

Energy-inefficient buildings could rapidly be exchanged for:

• Interchangeable buildings with living and housing tailored to the changing needs of different societies

- A second-hand market of plug-in structures

- Cities as collections of changeable cells

- A standardized set of over-the-counter building components

Add the global potential that the container network offers and there is a sense that a universal, off-the-peg structure and constructive blueprint could be created to meet the development needs of 99% of people.

Manufacturing

Buildings as consumer products are great news. It improves the quality of the built environment and reduces the cost and resources (including time) it takes to deliver. Precision manufactured buildings deliver improved sustainability and the design mantra "repair, re-use and recycle" lies at the heart of component sub-assembly.

There is a significant threat to note, however: due to the transportable nature of the shipping container, a significant number of jobs could be removed from local economies to the global manufacturing economies (currently predominant in the East).

However, as with every challenge, the flip side presents an opportunity. The construction industry has lots to learn from the lean manufacturing processes developed in the car and aviation industries. Efficient systems of component sub-assembly together with rising global fuel costs and competition for the transport network can mean that production facilities won't need to move offshore. Instead, production facilities can be housed at home in economies compliant with local rules and regulations. Structures as a consumer product mean that local resources are required to service operation and maintenance requirements including spare parts.

Design

A kit of globally transportable component parts would provide the tools for architects and designers to think differently about the same age-old problems.

Regeneration Tool

Using container architecture as a strategic tool for urban regeneration is where the most significant impact and results can be achieved.

The flexibility and versatility container architecture provides enables developers and communities to play and have fun. Container architecture provides the opportunity for trial and error, for experimentation and for a way out of stagnation.

The possibilities are endless: placemaking, decanting for refurbishment, affordable provision, feedback on design that does not need to be permanent, reduced timeframes, enhanced personal expression and personality of place with lower capital requirements. All these things make development more accessible to us all.

The future of container architecture

The projects featured in this book are a testament to the huge leap in creativity and innovation we have seen in container architecture in recent years.

But this is just the beginning.

Every day more and more container projects are being commissioned, developed and deployed as designers, companies and governments grow to understand the potential of a standardized and functional form of construction.

Entrepreneurs, designers, and disrupters will continue to challenge existing methods and ideas. Take the Pocket House featured on page x of this publication, a future when rather than moving home, we simply just move our home and follow, is within reach. At that point, when we can detach ourselves from land, we can truly start to engineer a sustainable presence.

The humble shipping container could truly disrupt a second industry and change the built landscape as we know it.

Chapter

01

Usages of
Container Buildings

Housing

Container buildings are mostly used for residential architecture. The compact furniture arrangement and the fact that the construction uses relatively little space are in accordance with the concept of land economization. Generally speaking, there are three different forms of residence.

First, container buildings can be used as temporary residences. Due to the ease of transportation, low cost, and high-quality compared to other temporary buildings, containers have particular advantage around construction sites and other non-permanent residences.

Second, containers can also be used as villas. In western countries, transforming containers into private homes is quite fashionable and already has been applied in practical use. Container villas are safe and comfortable for people to live in. With containers, not only detached villas can be constructed, but also other villas with more complicated structure.

Texas architect Jim Poteet designed a vacation cottage. The cottage was remodeled from a 40-foot (12-meter) container. The bathroom is located in the center, with a greenhouse on left and a living room on the right. Wide windows are used so that the living area is better integrated with the outside surroundings. The surface of the floor and the wall are made of bamboo panels.The cottage comes fully equipped with a heater, air conditioner, and sink.

Third, it can also be used as residential architecture. The containers can be stacked horizontally and vertically to form complex multi-layer or multi-unit container buildings as well as can be remodeled into compound large-scale residences.

Disaster Relief Housing

The Ex-Container project was designed to construct disaster relief container houses for the victims of Japanese tsunami in 2011. Victims may enjoy better living conditions in container buildings than other temporary architectures due to the relative cheap price. Given the short planning and implementation period required, container buildings would be a good choice for providing housing within the shortest time.

Standard containers are remodeled and combined to construct Ex-containers. It has been pointed out Japanese shipping containers by themselves can not be used as housing. Thus, it is important to remove unnecessary parts and redesign the building structure to conform with relevant regulations. In order to reduce the cost of the transportation of materials, work such as interior decoration and the exterior maintenance can be done beforehand in a factory. Then, semi-finished containers may later be directly transported to the site and assembled. Generally speaking, the expected usage period for the Ex-Container disaster relief housing is approximately two years. After this time, they could be further remodeled into common residences, further demonstrating the adaptability of container buildings.

Offices

Containers are a good choice for those companies who want their offices with unique industrialized look. With the combination of steel concrete structure and other supporting elements, the only difference between a container building and other conventional buildings may be distinctive wavy metal paneling on the outside. Consequently, the cost is remarkably reduced while still providing a high-quality space.

Because of the unstable nature of architectural projects ,buildings are confronted the possibility of being demolished within one or two years or even few months after being constructed. On the other hand, container architecture, unlike conventional architecture, can be recycled and reused, extending the material's usability.

For temporary offices, container buildings are unbeatable, especially in remote areas such as busy highways. Unlike brick and mortar buildings, container buildings can be transported directly to the site for immediate use, substantially reducing construction time. It is not unusual to see temporary container buildings along busy streets in parts of a city where particular importance has been attached to the urban environment.

Public Infrastructure and Commercial Facilities

Due to the compact structure and ease of transportation, containers have been widely used as public infrastructure in many cities. Facilities such as public washrooms, phone booths, and small retail shops are common to see along streets and in parks in the United States and various European countries. In China, containers are also usually converted into mini-supermarkets or newsstands.

Educational Facilities

The qualities of container buildings fit well with the style of the post-industrial era in cultural educational buildings. With the combination of modularity and coarse facade, these exquisite details make container architecture quite popular among young generations.

Throughout the world, several container art museums have been built and put into actual use, such as the Gwangju Museum of Art, the Seoul Arts Center, and Copenhagen Container Exhibition Center. The 53 Art Museum in Tianhe district of Guangzhou, China is another typical container museum.

These buildings present the beauty of postmodern aesthetics, which is warmly welcomed and highly praised by young adults.

The interior space of container buildings can also be used as classrooms. After the Wenchuan earthquake, CIMC built a new school building for Wenchuan Yanmen Primary School made out of containers. This is major application of containers in building educational facilities.

Scenic Buildings

As an industrial product, the pre-existing industrial characteristics of the containers are worked within the design, helping to complement industrial locations. The wineries in southern France are a good example of such an application, serving as a symbol of the regional culture and acting as a special expression of art.

Chapter

02

The Adaptive Design Combinations of Container Buildings

Containers can be used by themselves, but they can also be combined to create various kinds of buildings, all with the special features of containers. Container buildings can be categorized into three types: buildings converted from single container, buildings created from multiple containers, and buildings designed with containers and other materials.

Using different techniques to combine containers, modern container buildings offer great variety, from residence buildings to large-scale structures such as sports stadiums; from a single small container to a building built from hundreds of containers. Depending on the nature of the project, the size and the nature of the architecture can be different. It is safe to say that container design depends upon the limited space available. How much available space is there is a crucial factor in container design.

1. Non-Repetitive Container Design Combinations

In non-repetitive container design combinations, the constructive elements of the building are not repeated. In other words, the design is not the byproduct of any architectural element duplicated across the structure.

The diversity of such design combinations is the most interesting and adaptive ways of using containers. There are countless way of combining containers, but no matter how complicated the structure is, every design is based on basic components being fused together. Some common techniques include overlaying, staggering, and stacking.

1.1 Combining Containers Horizontally

1.1.1 Combining Closely Connected Containers

By placing containers next to one another, the interior space be enlarged to meet any spatial needs of the project. This is a good choice when single container does not provide sufficient space for the design and other means of extending the space.

If the containers are of a consistent length, a pattern can be created by placing containers length-wise. Dozens of spaces with different properties can be formed, sizes ranging from 297 square feet (27.6 square meters) to 900 square feet (83.6 square meters)(Figure 1).

Combination of 20-foot (6-meter) containers

Combination of 40-foot (12-meter) containers

20-foot (6-meter) container + 20-foot (6-meter) container = 297 square feet (27.6 square meters)

20-foot (6-meter) container + 40-foot (12-meter) container = 449 square feet (41.7 square meters)

Combination of 20-foot (6-meter) containers   Combination of 40-foot (12-meter) containers

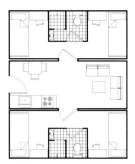

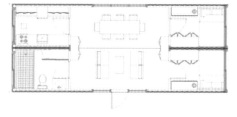

20-foot (6-meter) container + 20-foot (6-meter) container = 297 square   20-foot (6-meter) container + 20-foot (6-meter) container = 297 square
feet (27.6 square meters)   feet (27.6 square meters)

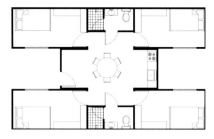

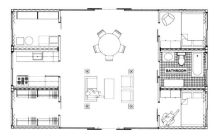

20-foot (6-meter)container + 40-foot (12-meter) container + 40-foot   40-foot (12-meter)container + 40-foot (12-meter) container + 40-foot
(12-meter) container = 748 square feet (69.5 square meters)   (12-meter) container = 900 square feet (83.6 square meters)

Figure 1. 20-foot containers (6-meter) and 40-foot (12-meter) container combinations

Horizontal combinations are not restricted to parallel or vertical combinations. Through proper renovation, more potential forms can be created. This method of combining applies to single-floor buildings as well as more complicated structures.

1.1.2 Design Combinations with Additions

By appending extra components to horizontally joined containers, even more space can be create as need by the project. In this fashion, these additions increase the physical area and overall adaptability of the project.

A project called Incubo House in Costa Rica consists of two 40-foot (12-meter) containers attached to a steel structure. On the floor, the containers and steel work are connected, while on the rooftop, there is a highly elevated clerestory. Cross-ventilation in the building eliminates the need for air-conditioning and natural light virtually eliminates the need for electrical lighting during the day.

Stanco Paul designed his own private residence by appending components to shipping containers.Two 20-foot (6-meter) containers are placed horizontally with a wooden structure in between. The corners of the wooden structure fit right on top of the containers, making a smooth slope that ensures rainwater slides off. The side plating is further appended with additional plywood and a wooden box consisting of per-fabricated facilities such as windows and doors.. The space between the two containers is used as living room, while the interior of the containers is consist of a bedroom, storeroom, washroom and other areas.

The Y Container Experimental Residence was a project built by students from Tongji University for 2011 Solar Decathlon in the United States. The building is made up of six 20-foot (6-meter) containers. Two container are bonded together as a single unit, forming a Y shape. The triangular area in the middle is a mix of glass and steel work.

1.2 Combining Containers Vertically

1.2.1 Stacking Containers Vertically

Stacking containers is most common method in vertical design. With the advantage of fast and efficient construction, combination of this kind can make the best use of the container's modular qualities (Figure 2). The height of a single container is 8.5 feet (2.59 meters), while two containers have a height of 17 feet (5.18 meters), and three containers 24.5 feet (7.77 meters). This is the standard way to estimate the height of a container building built with stacked containers.

Figure 2.

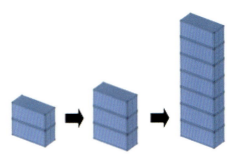

Figure 2. Containers stacked vertically

A beachfront apartment near the port of Yokohama is an good example of a design stacking two containers. Each unit consists of two containers stacked upon one another. The entrance is in the middle of the base. Living room, entrance and the bathroom are located on the first floor and the bedroom is set on the second floor. The corners of the containers have been firmly fixed by bolts and the two containers in each unit have been further reinforced together with a concrete baseplate. The bolts and the baseplate can always be dismantled, making the container building highly recyclable as well.

Ross Stevens designed and built a container residence in New Zealand designed using a vertical stack of three 40-foot (12-meter) containers. The space between containers is utilized as well to maximize the space. The base steel frame serves as garage, which rests underneath the stack of containers. A staircase runs from the base and the upper container, making the most of the residual space in the building.

Freitag's flagship store in Zurich (Figure 3) is another example of vertical stacking in design . The building is an asymmetric tower of nine 20-foot (6-meter) containers with a total height of 65.6 feet (21.2 meters), rising from a 13×6.5 feet (4×2 meters) base. The first two floors of the store consist of four shipping containers each, while the third and the fourth floors have two containers each and the rest of the floors are just one container each. The deceasing number of the containers from bottom to the top gives a sense of stability. The top four containers had their siding on the north end removed to create large space of 15.4 feet (4.7 meter) in height and 15.2 feet (4.7 meters) in width. This is now used as sales outlet, reception desk and exhibition area. The vertical section of four containers are used as show rooms. The staircase and the emergency escape are close to the external wall to the south for easy access. On the top floor, there is an observation deck that enable tourists to admire beautiful landscape of Zurich. However, this pre-fabricated structure lacks sense of integrity. Consequently, the containers were welded to one another and tie rods were attached to the outer wall to further increase stability. What is interesting about the design is that the two extra containers on the first and second floor, not only enlarges the space but also integrates with the original building. Furthermore, this approach increases growth capacity of the container building in a way that can hardly be found in other more convetional buildings.

1.2.2. Staggered Vertical Placement of Containers

In vertical design combinations, staggered vertical placement also is quite common design. In this case, both the height of the house and the functionality can be amplified. Unlike designs where containers are joined end to end, in a staggered design, the placement is not fixed.

Figure 3.

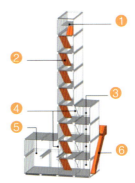

1 Sightseeing platform
2 Straight-run staircase
3 Four-floor
4 Reinforcement structure
5 Entrance
6 Outdoor staircase

Figure 3 Freitag flagship store in Zurich

Figure 4.

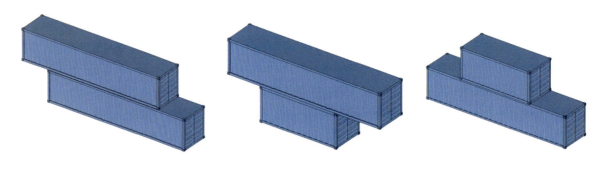

Figure 4 Three basic staggered formations

There are three basic formations for staggered placement (Figure 4):

(a) When the upper and the lower container are of the same size, outdoor terrace be created from the upper container cantilevering the lower one.

(b) When the upper container is longer than the lower one, neither side or just one side may be fixed to the corners of the lower container, leaving the rest of the container cantilevering off the side.

(c) When the upper container is shorter than the lower, outdoor terrace could be formed.

These three basic formations can be evolved to create even more forms .

Three 20-foot (6-meter) containers have been placed in a staggered fashion (Figure 5). Vertical transportation within the building can be achieved by an exterior staircase, and people can enter through an outdoor terrace on each flight of the stairs. Likewise, the interior of the container can be arranged into different functional spaces.

LOT-EK used 24 40-foot (12-meter) shipping containers to construct PUMA City in Boston. A three-story stack of containers creates internal and outdoor spaces, large overhangs, as well as terraces.The building consists of two retail spaces on the lower levels, both designed with double-height ceilings and wide open space,contrasting with the compact qualities of the container. The entrance of the building is located in the gray area in the middle of the bottom floor. Both the outdoor and the inner staircase be use to move throughout the building. Given the cantilevered structure and use of containers, the building is representative of the post-industrial age.

Another example of staggered design is a detached villa designed by Meta made up of four containers. The containers are arranged in staggered fashion and bamboo laminate is used as the external wall. Grey space on the first floor and the roof deck on the second floor increase the practicality of the building.

Several containers need to be combined together by dismantling adjacent siding to enlarge the indoor net area in this staggered placement. If necessary, additional columns should be added to reinforce the structure. The following pictures from A to E are five ways to install additional columns. The additional columns are represented by red dotted lines.

Figure 5.

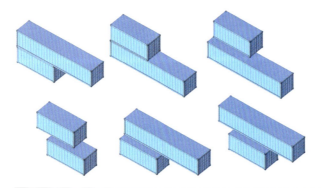

Figure 5. Other evolutionary formations in container box up-and-down parallel staggered placement

Figure 6.

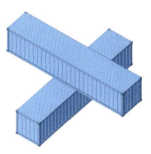

Figure 6. Container vertical cross-staggered placement

1.2.3. Cross-Staggered Vertical Placement

Cross-staggered vertical placement is another way to create more space as well as a more interesting shape for the building (Figure 6).

There are two ways to deal with transportation within the building with cross-staggered placement. One is to stack two containers on top of one another then build external stairway. In this case, the path to the second floor can also function as an outdoor terrace. In such a situation, the upper container would be best placed in the center of the building, while entrances on the terrace and structural reinforcement should be designed according to figures 5 and 6.

Another way of allowing transportation inside the building is to place the staircases within the overlapping section of the two stacked containers, With this method, various combinations can be formed through staggered placement. (Figure 7)

The method of vertical staggered placement was applied in the construction of the Bretagne container residence. The cantilevered section on the second floor holds the bedroom while the two containers on the first floor hold dining room and living room.

If the steel siding is removed, additional column should be added to the container. Figure 8 illustrates how to properly install additional columns according to relative position of the containers. The additional columns are represented by red dotted lines.

1.2.4 Large-Span Space Created by Combining Containers

The upper container is stacked across the corner ends of lower containers. Two or more containers are at the bottom to support the load of the upper container, together forming a large-span area. (Figure 9).

Various different methods of combing containers, such as simple stacking or other more complicated methods, can be used to construct buildings with many different spans (Figure 10).

Figure 7.

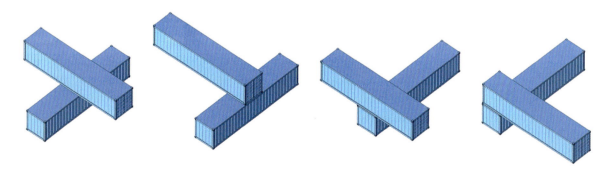

Figure 7. Cross-staggered placement

Figure 8.

Facade   Lateral view   Facade   Lateral view

Figure 8. Proper installation of additional columns for staggered container placement

Figure 9.

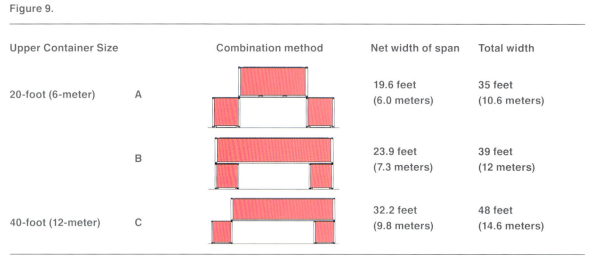

Upper Container Size		Combination method	Net width of span	Total width
20-foot (6-meter)	A		19.6 feet (6.0 meters)	35 feet (10.6 meters)
	B		23.9 feet (7.3 meters)	39 feet (12 meters)
40-foot (12-meter)	C		32.2 feet (9.8 meters)	48 feet (14.6 meters)

Figure 9. Large-span space created by combining containers

Figure 10.

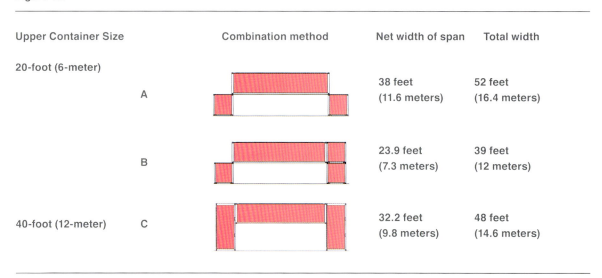

Upper Container Size		Combination method	Net width of span	Total width
20-foot (6-meter)	A		38 feet (11.6 meters)	52 feet (16.4 meters)
	B		23.9 feet (7.3 meters)	39 feet (12 meters)
40-foot (12-meter)	C		32.2 feet (9.8 meters)	48 feet (14.6 meters)

Figure 10. Table of various combinations of large-span container buildings

Figure 11.

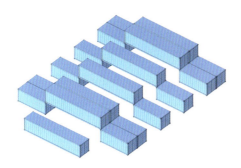

Figure 11. Bernardes Jacobsen Container Art Gallery

The span length can be adjusted to 4 feet (1.2 meters) in length and 20 feet (6 meters) in width when 20-foot upper container is used. Whereas, the span length can be increased to 24 feet (7.3meters) in length and 39 feet (12 meters) in width if the size of the upper container is doubled. The span length and width of the arch are primarily decided by different functions of the building.

Special attention should be paid to column F of figure 10 since its construction is different from the other columns. In columns from A to E, the upper container is placed on top of the lower containers. In column F, however, the upper container is lodged between the two sides of the lower containers. Methods such as welding and anchoring should be taken to fix the upper container in place. Steel brackets should be installed in advance on the two sides to support the upper container.

The entrance of the Bernardes Jacobsen Container Art Gallery is a good example that the method in column A . The span entrance created by a 20-foot container is a two-story semi-open building. As shown in column E of figure 10, the upper container is 40 feet (12 meters) and the lower containers are 20 feet (6 meters). In total, six containers are staggered to construct the external space of the Bernardes Jacobsen Container Art Gallery.

In Quik Build Ecosystem(QBE), as shown in column B of Figure 10, five 40-foot containers and   40-foot containers form the large-span space below.

1.2.5 Stacking Containers at Oblique Angles

Stacking upper and lower containers at oblique angles is rare to see in container building. Theoretically, the concept of is not compatible with container design, but with special structural treatment, containers can still adapt to different spatial and function requirements . It is very important to handle the spatial and angular adjustment carefully.

The method of stacking upper and lower containers at oblique angles was used in building the ECO-Cargo container residence. Much like in picture (b) of figure 12, two corner columns are placed diagonally. The entrance hall, the studio the bathroom are on the first floor, while the bedroom and the dining room are on the second floor. Vertical transportation was established within the horizontally overlapping project in the building. The exterior terrace on the second floor is covered by other materials and is used as part of the interior space.1.3 Comprehensive Design Combinations

In constructing buildings, different methods such as vertical and horizontal placement, can be used together to create

Figure 12.

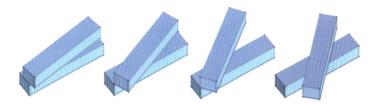

Figure 12. Stacking containers at oblique angles

rather complicated independent structures. As a result, container buildings are usually large in space and vary greatly in shape and style. Generally speaking, there are three types of comprehensive design combinations.

1.3.1 Coordinating Container Design with Other Structures

For the structural design, additional architectural components, such as steel or concrete reinforcement, might be needed to fulfill the spatial and functional demands of the project.

Twelve 20-foot containers were combined to create the Adriance container residence in nothern Maine. Containers were partially used for the structure to support a glossy glass that envelops the house. The kitchen and the living area are partially enclosed within shipping container. Two steel staircases lead to the second floor of container where the bedroom is situated. Exterior structures that are supported by short columns are placed on top on the container. The whole space is nearly 4000 square feet (1200 square meters) with a double-height garage door opening connecting the interior of the building with the exterior (Figure 13).

Another example is the hybrid ecological residence designed by ecotechdesign, located in the desert area near Los Angeles. Recycled containers were used for refurbishment and modeling. Pipe installation, heating equipment installation, as well as bathroom and kitchen remodeling was all prefabricated in Los Angeles and transported to the project location for assembly. Bolted joints were used to reinforce the steel structure. Perforated metal plates and solar panels play an important part in providing shade and managing internal temperature. Moreover, sustainable water-saving equipment was also installed.

1.3.2 Large-scale Buildings Principally Using Containers

The Forks apartment designed by MWBa mainly consists of nine 40-foot (12-meter) container and one 20-foot (6-meter) container. The containers are vertically stacked three stories high to form two units with a gap of 3.9 feet (1.2 meters) in between. Concrete, glass and other components were employed to enlarge the interior space. The garage on the first floor is about 1184 square feet (110 square meters) and the total living area on the second and the third floor is 2465 square feet (229 square meters). Additional structures were used to construct the terrace, the balcony, the staircase, and other facilities. Load calculations were taken into consideration to ensure safety issues were avoided.

The'GAD' Contemporary Art Gallery in Oslo, Norway was designed by MMW in 2005. Given the semi-permanent and movable nature of container construction and assembly, the gallery could be disassembled and reassembled in mere few days. The 'GAD' gallery is made up of ten 40-foot (12-meter) standard freight containers. The main first floor gallery space consists of three closely placed containers. The second floor uses three containers to create a U-shape.One container is parallel with the base and the other two are cantilevered off the base and supported by two steel columns below each container. This U-shape form wraps around the central terrace on the second floor, which can be reached by a steel staircase. On the third floor, an elevated exhibition room provides an access to the rooftop. In addition, a large transitional space is reserved for gatherings and events. The design breaks the traditional closed-box concept, turning the gallery into an open and multi-functional place of recreation.

The container office in Rhode Island was designed by distill studio. It is a building of 12 offices built from 32 recycled containers. Part of the indoor walls was removed to create a wide and open space. The three-story building is divided into two sections, which are connected by a two-story overbridge. The two sections look practically identical from the external facade. A steel staircase at the main entrance leads to a terrace on the second floor, which provides access to the third floor. A metal canopy in the center of the building on the second floor protects and shades the inner space during the summer. Solar panels are placed on the top of the canopy for sustainable energy . The industrial nature of the container is presented through the smart use of methods such as overlaying and cantilevering. 1.3.3 Enclosed Large-scale Interior Space Design Combinations

Figure 13.

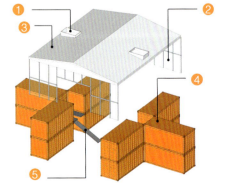

1 Daylight opening
2 Glass curtain wall
3 Steel deck roof
4 20-foot (6-meter) standard container
5 Additional steel staircase

Figure 13. Adriance container residence

Figure 14.

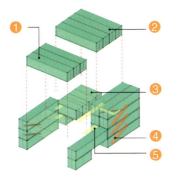

1 40-foot (12-meter) standard container as roofing structure
2 40-foot (12-meter) standard container as roofing structure
3 40-foot (12-meter) standard container as cantilever structure
4 Additional staircase
5 Additional corridor

Figure 14. Platoon Kunsthalle Exhibit Hall and Art Center

1.3.3 Enclosed Large-scale Interior Space Design Combinations

1. Container as large-span structure

As shown in figure 10, the span of a 40-foot freight container, which ranges from 24 feet (7.3 meters) to 39 feet (12 meters), is wide enough to meet the requirements of various functional spaces in both ordinary and large-scale buildings.

Platoon Kunsthalle Exhibit Hall and Art Center in Berlin, Germany was designed and built by Graft Lab Architects in 2009. Plantoon Kunshalle is made up of 28 ISO cargo containers. The containers play a central role in the structure. The 40-foot (12-meter) containers are placed on top to form the roofing structure. As column E of figure 10 shows, the roof spans about 38.7 feet (11.8 meters). The prefabricated 20-foot (6-meter) containers that project out into the interior space are used as functional rooms. Steel bridging pieces were added sparsely throughout as corridors to facilitate traffic. Double-glazed glass was installed at the spaces between containers on the roof to make the interior well lit by natural light (Figure 14).

The Gwangju Museum of Art has a space of 10,968 square feet (1019 square meters). It was built with 25 40-foot (12-meter) containers and four 20-foot (6-meter) ISO containers. The large-span container structure is the same as the structure shown in column C of figure 10. The large open space in the center has a span of about 32 feet (9.8 meters), a width of about 19.5 meters), and a height of about 16.7feet (5.1 meters). Generally, the space can be used as a movie theater, exhibition hall other functional spaces. The large-span 40-foot container (12-meter) on the roof also can be used as additional room as circumstances require.Extra containers were set around the space outside to form an enclosed courtyard (Figure 15).

2. Containers as Vertical Bracing in Large-span Structures

A simple and convenient container combination can act as the vertical bracing in a large-span structure, replacing traditional pillar support. This design facilitates the construction and alleviates the effort need on building the pillar foundation. Containers can be placed and arranged both vertically and horizontally (Figure 16).

Figure 15.

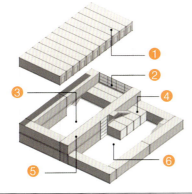

1 The 32-foot (9.8-meter) roof span of the 40-foot standard container
2 Glass curtain wall
3 20-foot (6-meter) standard container room units
4 Central space
5 40-foot (12-meter) standard container as supporting structure
6 Outdoor courtyard

Figure 15. Gwangju Museum of Art

Figure 16.

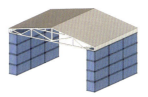

Figure 16. Container as vertical bracing in large-span structure

Built in 2004, the Cruise Center in Hamburg, Germany is a three-story container building,   measuring 220.11 feet (67.09 meters) in length, 75.8 feet (23.1 meters) in width, with a total area of 17,115 square feet (1590 square meters). The span of the structure is about 60 feet (18.3 meters), which is equal to the length of three 20-foot (6-meter) containers. The truss-frame structure and translucent material are used on the top so that the building presents its special and distinctive features when light illuminates the rooftop at night. The containers were used as the vertical bracing for structure as well as functioned as the building enclosure.

Designed by Japanese architect Shigeru Ban, The Nomadic Museum is the largest mobile museum in the world. Twenty-foot (six-meter) containers that were placed horizontally and arranged in picturesque disorder acted as the vertical bracing for the large-span structure. The Nomadic Museum consists of three sections: the wall, the roof, and the pillar. The wall is a group of staggered containers with the hollow interior covered by a thin film. The roof, an aluminum truss, is also covered with a thin film material. The pillar is a series of paper tubes measuring 32.8-foot (10-meter) in length and 24.3-foot (7.4-meter) in diameter that support the roof.

The New York Nomadic Museum was built with 148 containers with a total length of 672.6 feet (205 meters). It covers a total area of 57,048 square feet (5300 square meters), including galleries, cinemas, museums and shops. The building's space can be further extended by adding more containers to the original structure.

2. Repetitive Container Design Combinations

Individual container units are used as the spatial and functional elements of the building. The container units in the building are similar in function, placement and arrangement. Therefore, individual container units are repeated elements in design.The interior layout of the container unit plays an important part in repetive modular container design combinations. The positions of door and window openings as well as the other layout possibilities have been previously introduced. Adjustments, such as refining the internal means of transportation, should be taken into consideration based on how the containers are combined. Consequently, repetitive container design combinations is an iterative process of adapting the layout to suit the needs of the project.

2.1 Veranda-style Structure

Without the need for additional separation, renovation, or trimming, veranda-style container design combinations is the most common form of repetitive container combination. Furthermore, the method fits best with prefabricated assembling, which is what containers excel at . There are several ways of container layout for the veranda-style structure. As figure 17 shows, there are three main ways to combine containers and additional structures to create a veranda-style   design. In figure 17 A, without using any extra structural support, an interior traffic corridor is formed through cutting and dismantling the siding on one end and setting additional walls to the containers. In figure 17 B, additional corridors and vertical supporting structures are used to create a traffic corridor with access to each container unit. Minimal modification to the containers is needed in this way. In figure 17 C, the containers are vertically placed, with the indoor floor traffic space as well as part of the vertical support in each unit coming from additional structures.

With a total area of 33,3681 square feet (31,000 square meters), Keetwonen student dormitory in The Netherlands is the biggest container building in the world. It is a five-story container building with auxiliary facilities. The building is made up of 1034 independent container units. In each container unit, a separate bathroom space divides the long container into the two parts: the kitchen and the living area. In each unit, the sleeping and the rest area, the workspace, and the balcony are provide with adequate lighting as well as good acoustic and thermal insulation. One building unit can be sub-divided into four parts: the 40-foot (12-meter) containers, the balcony, the corridor (Figure 17 picture B), and the sloping roof structure. The containers are stacked five stories high. The balcony and the traffic corridor are connected to the containers on one end and supported by an independent lightweight steel structure one the other end as well as by a diagonal bar at the bottom. The staircase functions as a connecting corridor between the two buildings.

Figure 17.

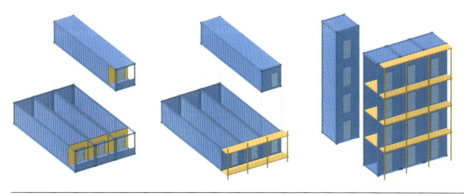

Figure17. Veranda-style container designs and transportation system (Structural additions in yellow and original container in blue)

Founded by the Green Container International Rescue Foundation, the Haitian Container Collections is a unique container building outfitted with an external corridor. The 40-foot (12-meter) containers in the south are cantilevered off the base to create a chic yet rhythmic appearance. On the north side of the building, A steel structure has been added to function as a long corridor and an outdoor staircase arranged at the end of the building. The thermal insulation on the pitched roof is supported by short columns placed on top of the containers.

In Onagawa, Shigeru Ban Architects built a temporary container housing complex using 189 containers, all stacked in a checkerboard pattern three stories high. The entire residential community within the complex consists of nine container residences. Each container residences is made up of 24 containers. Because of the checkerboard pattern, both the interior and the exterior space of the containers can be put to good use. Spaces between the containers are fully exploited to provide parking area, living area, and community facilities. According to the container arrangement, four different housing types were planed and designed to meet the needs of different families. The staircase is arranged at the two ends of each container unit and a long outer corridor is also installed for transportation.

The Ursula Hall-Laurus Wing container student dormitory at Australian National University in Canberra was built in 2010 by Quicksmart. The six-story dormitory was built with 204 prefabricated container units. There are three different housing types within building: one type of single room and two types of suites. The project does not have an independent external corridor supporting the structure. Rather, much like in figure 17 B, the containers were combined after the removal of siding on one end, with a balcony built in on the other end. With a few additional components, prefabricated containers can be lifted on and off of the stack, helping to shorten the construction period.

The container dormitory in the Vanke Architectural Research Center was designed by Mick Pierce. The containers were vertically placed with corridors and floor structures later added on. This makes good use of the advantages of independent vertical structures in avoiding problems such as building too high or too wide with the container placement.

Each vertically placed container is separated into four floors. With a net use area of 59.95 square feet (5.57 square meters), each floor within the container can be used as an independent bedroom unit (Figure 18 C). Container suites are comprised of four to six containers and are arranged in a circular pattern. The looping exterior corridor is placed in this enclosed circular pattern for transportation (Figure 18 A).

Due to the limited interior space of individual containers, numerous individual containers are always combined into container suites to adequately fit families of various sizes (Figure 18 E-G). The spatial arrangement of individual containers is often influenced by certain functions and facilities, such as the drainage system. A veranda structure is used in connecting the looping exterior corridor with the container suites. Spatial arrangement of this kind plays an important role in enhancing the functional adaptability of modular containers.

Figure 18.

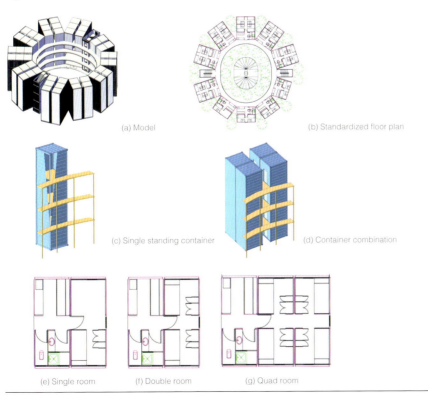

(a) Model

(b) Standardized floor plan

(c) Single standing container

(d) Container combination

(e) Single room   (f) Double room   (g) Quad room

Figure 18 The container dormitory of vanke Architectural Research Center

Figure 19.

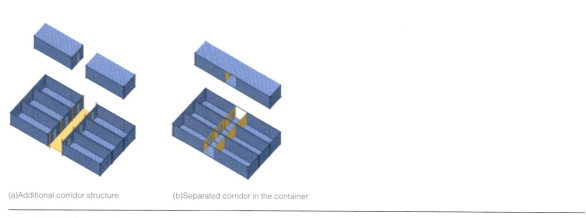

(a)Additional corridor structure   (b)Separated corridor in the container

Figure 19. Two basic types of interior corridors

2.2 The Composition of Interior Corridors

There are two major uses for an interior corridor: one is to be used as the traffic space within the interior of the container, the other is to complement other structures, such as lightweight steel reinforcement or concrete plating (Figure 19). Besides the additional structure necessary in constructing a veranda design, the design for interior corridors is basically the same as veranda design. It should be noted that additional support would be needed when containers are combined (Figure 20).

The Qubic container student apartment complex in Amsterdam was built in 2005. There are 715 student apartment units in this three-story building. Each story is made up of three 20-foot (6-meter) containers. The container in the middle of the three is used as a traffic corridor and toilet facility with access to the two living areas on both sides. When the prefabricated containers are assembled and combined, parts of the containers were removed to make place for a hanging garden. Each external wall of the container is covered with plexiglass and plastic decorative paneling. Six different colors are repeated in a seemingly random fashion on all the facades to add a sense of whimsy to the entire building.

Figure 20.

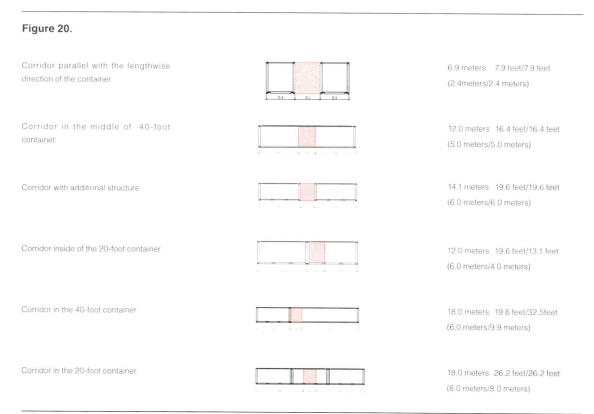

Corridor parallel with the lengthwise direction of the container		6.9 meters 7.9 feet/7.9 feet (2.4meters/2.4 meters)
Corridor in the middle of 40-foot container		12.0 meters 16.4 feet/16.4 feet (5.0 meters/5.0 meters)
Corridor with additional structure		14.1 meters 19.6 feet/19.6 feet (6.0 meters/6.0 meters)
Corridor inside of the 20-foot container		12.0 meters 19.6 feet/13.1 feet (6.0 meters/4.0 meters)
Corridor in the 40-foot container		18.0 meters 19.6 feet/32.5feet (6.0 meters/9.9 meters)
Corridor in the 20-foot container		18.0 meters 26.2 feet/26.2 feet (8.0 meters/8.0 meters)

Figure 20. Table showing different forms of interior corridors

The Yenagoa Hotel in Nigeria was designed by Tempohousing in 2009. Using container construction techniques, this project was constructed quickly in unfavorable construction conditions during the rainy season. A prefabricated system made out of 168 40-foot (12-meter) containers was used to build guest houses. The four-story building is connected with an internal-corridor that is formed from partially dismantling the containers in the middle of the building. There are 144 standard suites, each with the size of 280 square feet (26 square meters), and 12 presidential suites, each with the size of 560 square feet (52 square meters). The interior of the suite is made from combining two adjacent containers and removing the metal siding.

The NDSM container dormitories in The Netherlands (Figure 21) were built with 380 20-foot (6-meter) containers. The staircase and the independent inner walkway in this three-story building are made of perforated metal plating, allowing ventilation with the windows in the opposite corridor. Containers are painted in different four colors: red, white, blue and orange. All of the painted containers were arranged randomly to enrich visual appearance of the facade.

2.3 The Composition of Non-corridor Structures

Proyecto, a five-story container house in Tocopilla, Chile was designed by Emilio Ugart. A central open staircase connects the whole building and is accessible to the residents on both two sides. A single unit is a combination of a 40-foot (12-meter) container and a 20-foot (6-meter) container, with an interior space of 474 square feet (44 square meters). The 20-foot (6-meter) container was staggered with the 40-foot container (12-meter), which is cantilevered off the base and used to create a balcony. The top of the container provides an outdoor terrace for the residents upstairs. An amazingly unique building has been created all by making full use of the container's structure and artful cantilevering of the containers.

The Cité A Docks is a container student dormitory by the seaside in Le Havre, France. Using a metal grid, the containers were renovated into a four-story building holding a hundred apartments, each with a size of 258 square feet (24 square meters). The metal frame provides structural support for the containers and makes space for aisles, terraces, and balconies. Instead of a long corridor shared by the whole building, two to three units share one vertical staircase with an access to the rooms. The first floor is raised off the ground to guarantee the same level of privacy in each room and a huge glass wall lets in the natural light. The prison atmosphere and the uniform space prevalent in dormitories are abandoned and, instead, the building boasts a facade both open feeling and welcoming.

3.1 Analysis of Single Container Interior Layout Design

The layout of the interior of a single container varies according to different functional properties that are needed. Common indoor building functions of a residence include: bathroom, kitchen, bed, writing desk, and various storage spaces. Due to the restrictions in piping construction, showers, sinks, toilets, and other facilities requiring water cannot be moved while they are in use. Therefore, such facilities have a great influence on the layout and a qualitative analysis of container interior layout can be done based on the spatial properties and the position of such facilities.

Figure 22 is a statistical analysis of a 20-foot (6-meter) container residence interior layout. From this figure, we can see that when the entrance is set at the end of the container and fixed facilities, such as the kitchen and the toilet, are set near the entrance, you can get a larger internal space with an obvious spatial transition from public to private areas.

On the other hand, if the fixed facilities are installed far away from the entrance, the natural light at the end of the container can hardly been taken full advantage of and additional windows opening on the sides would be needed for indoor illumination. When the entrance is set in the middle of the container, fixed facilities can also be placed near the entrance. In this situation, two independent spaces can be formed at the opposite ends of the container and can be used as two separate spaces.

Figure 21.

Figure 21.The NDSM container dormitories in the Netherlands axis plan

Figure 22.

Position of the entrance	Layout of 20-foot (6-meter) container	Combination scheme

Entrance at the end of the container

Direction

The open area near the entrance is designed to be the kitchen with access to the bathroom, while the habitable area as a whole stays intact and independent. The functional division of the room is quite obvious. Windows are at the two ends of the container, so that containers can be easily joined together.

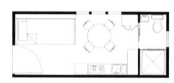

The entrance is a narrow passage, with the bathroom on one side of the passage. The simple kitchen is located in the bedroom, which might impact daily life.

The windows, which are on the sides of the container, potentially limit container combinations.

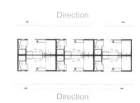

The entrance leads directly to the habitable space and the kitchen, which might have impact daily life. At the end of the container is the bathroom. In this case, the habitable area is maximized. The windows are located on three sides of the container, which might reduce options for combining containers.

Entrance in the middle of the container

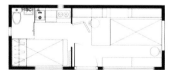

Direction

Direction

The living room is opposite to the entrance. A double bed is placed at the end of the container to improve the comfort level of the accomodation. The bathroom is at the other end of the container. The window and the entrance are on the same side so that the containers could be combined horizontally.

The whole space is divided in to a primary and a secondary space by a door. The primary habitable space is on the right of the entrance, while the secondary living space consisting of a single bed, bathroom, and kitchen is on the left. The windows and the doors are located on all four sides. As a result, it is impossible to closely combined with other containers.

Position of the entrance	Layout of 20-foot (6-meter) container	Combination scheme

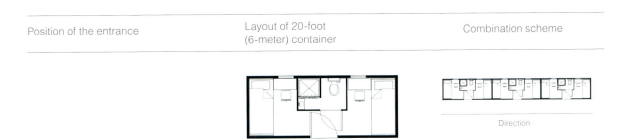

Direction

The whole container space is divided into two sections with the bathroom in the middle. The spaces on either sides are independent habitable spaces that would have no potential interference. The window and the door are on only two sides of the container which means that the containers can be combined horizontally.

Figure 22. Possible interior layouts of 20-foot (6-meter) container residence

In the 20-foot (6-meter) container accommodations sold by Stankey container company in the United States, the entrance is placed at the end of the container and all spatial division is already done in advance.

The kitchen and the storage room are near the entrance, all of which connect to the habitable area by a corridor. In the habitable area, a bed, table and chairs are hidden in a side wall, which can be pulled out or stored away as needed. This design guarantees the integrity of the interior and makes good use of the container's inherent customizability.

3.2 Designing Spatial Extensions for Containers

In spite of the fact that the container building has many positive features such as flexibility, convenience, mobility, and adaptability, it cannot be denied that it is restricted by its limited and narrow interior space. Therefore, some means of extension are effective ways to augment the internal space of the container and to increase the adaptability of the building for different functions.

3.2.1 Retractable Extension

California Institute of Technology designed and built a container building that can be augmented in size by extending the space of the container. A standard 20-foot (6-meter) container can be expanded by opening the front door of the container and pulling out an8 feet×8 feet (2.4 ×2.4 meters) internal space along a track. Built-in boxes hidden in the container could also be pulled out through the openings on the sides for further space. Through retractable extension, the size of the original container is significantly enlarged from 148.65 square feet (13.81 square meters) to around 258 square feet (24 square meters) (Figure 23).

LOT-EK designed a series of mobile residential units, each built from a 40-foot (12-meter) freight container. Each unit contains a separate module for various functional areas, such as kitchen, bathroom, bedroom, studio, and so on. These modules are installed in the container during transportation. On the arrival to the destination, the functional modules slide out of the container and spread out. The functional modules are clearly delineated. The interior center is a complete and spacious area that can be used to hold various activities. Using retractable extensions, the space is maximized in the single container and is enlarged by 224.43 square feet (20. 85 square meters), almost a 75% increase in size (Figure 24).

Figure 23.

Figure 23.Spatial extension design

Figure 24.

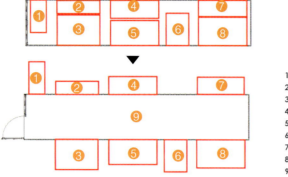

1 Cupboard
2 Kitchen
3 Dining room
4 Sofa
5 Studio
6 Closet
7 Bathroom
8 Bedroom
9 Activity space

Figure 24. Extension of mobile residential units

3.3 Case Studies of Space Usage Within Single Containers

A single container can also be used as the basic unit in the construction of a combined container building or a large-scale container building.

In the container student dormitory in Australian National University, 40-foot (12-meter) standard freight containers were used as individual rooms of the building. Each room is fully equipped with general necessities: induction cooker, microwave oven, refrigerator, sink, and other equipment items in the kitchen area; bookcase, desk, chair, and internet connection in the working area; a single bed, storage space under the bed, and dresser in the bedroom. In addition, heating, television, telephone are also provided. In order to diversify the units available, two single containers are combined to extend the space and expand functionality. A door is installed in the side wall of the container near the corridor. For convenience of maintenance, the bathroom is placed near the entrance and the pipes are installed near the corridor. The middle of the container is designed for the kitchen facilities and writing desk. It is a spacious area with small tables and chairs around in circle for meals. The bedroom is on the other side of the container far from the corridor. A bookcase is suspended above the bed. A small balcony in the middle of the container integrates nature with the building, playing an important role in providing shade.

Designed by French architects Olgga, Crou is a student dormitory made from 100 used containers stacked together. In this design, each unit is made up of 40-foot containers (12-meter) with an entrance on both the end and one of the sides of the container.

By designing the space with the entrance at the end, the space near the entrance is a separate dining space equipped with kitchen facilities and a dining table. The bathroom, which includes a toilet and shower stall, is in the middle and water tanks are placed in an adjacent space on the wall. The dim lighting conditions deep in container makes it an appropriate place for the bedroom, while the space on the opposite end with a large French window is a perfect place for the studio.

Taken into consideration the needs of those in wheelchairs, all the furniture is placed on one side of the space to widen the traffic space as much as possible. The kitchen, the home appliances, and the dining table are opposite to the entrance. The dining space and a particularly spacious bathroom big enough for a wheelchair are on the left side of the entrance while the desk, bookcase, and dresser are on right side of the entrance. The bed is on one side of the container near the window. The side entrance maximizes the traffic space and minimizes the space occupied by a fixed cabinet.

Temperhousing has designed a range of container building units: double corridor, central corridor, and dipteral. Several different models of container buildings can be formed and developed, each with different facilities and space.

A double corridor container unit is a 40-foot (12-meter) container used as a separate interior suite. By placing the entrance on the end, the entrance and a floor-to-ceiling window or a balcony can be on opposite ends of the container. Pipes, sanitary facilities and kitchen equipment are located in the middle of the container (Figure 25).

A central corridor container unit is built from a 40-foot (12-meter) container with one of the side walls partly sliced in the middle to be used as a corridor. The container is divided into two separate unit spaces which are located on both sides of the corridor respectively. Similar to the layout of a hotel room, the bathroom is near the entrance and the bed is in the middle or at the end of each container. After combining with several identical containers, a single container can support a corridor without additional reinforcement (Figure 26).

A dipteral container unit is is a 40-foot (12-meter) container divided into two separate rooms with a separation in the middle. Each of the rooms can be entered from both ends of the container. With just the removal of original metal

Figure 25.

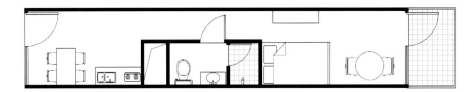

Figure 25. Double corridor container model

Figure 26.

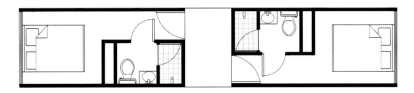

Figure 26. Central corridor container model

components and the installment of windows and doors at both ends, this can maintain the basic structure of the container, facilitating the refurbishment of the dormitory. This is more economical and convenient compared to double corridor container units. The double-corridor container unit can be further divided into complete separation and the partial separation of the internal space. In a partially separated container unit with double corridor, a single 40-foot (12-meter) container can be modified into a space that can house two people. The entrances are located at opposite ends of the container while a shared bathroom is in the middle. Each person has his or hers own bedroom, kitchen, and other facilities. Privacy can be guaranteed with locks on the two door that lead to the central bathroom (Figure 27).

A 40-foot (12-meter) container can used in a completely separated unit with double corridor as well. Entrances are located on both ends of the container, with pipeline equipment in an enclosed space in the middle separating the two. Each room is equipped with its own bathroom and kitchen (Figure 28)

Figure 27.

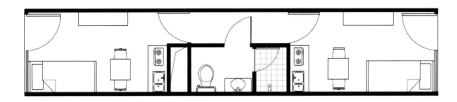

Figure 27. Partially separated double corridor container unit

Figure 28.

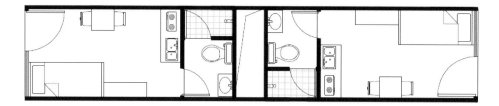

Figure 28. Complete Separated double corridor container unit

Chapter

03

Basic Modification Procedures for Container Building Construction

1. The Basic Steps in Container Building Construction

Although the construction of container buildings is complex and different from that of conventional structures, there are still some things in common between the two regarding design. Generally speaking, the following basic steps should always be taken (Figure 29).

1. Examine the estimated space requirement for the building. Make sure the architectural design and layout takes into account the interior space of a container after renovation.

2. Make preliminary study on various sizes and models of container, to find the type that best suits your project.

3. Renovate the purchased containers, polishing off rusty section of the container, coating the container with anti-rust paint, and spraying the surface with thermal insulation.

4. Dismantle the metal body of the container according to design, cutting out openings for doors and windows in the container.

5. Add a steel structure to wherever structural reinforcement is needed.

6. Weld the door frames and the windows into the cut-off sections of the container. Weld the internal frame.

7. Install thermal insulation.

8. Install wiring, water supply and drainage pipes.

9. Install fixed furniture for bathroom, kitchen, and bedroom.

10. Install decorative paneling for the walls and ceiling.

11. Select and install the appropriate flooring.

12. Address details such as the installation of lamps and arrangement of furniture.

Figure 29.

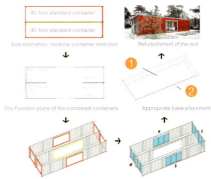

1 Concrete slab with rammed earth below
2 Strip foundation

Figure 29. Steps in modifying a container for construction
Source: sketch based on information from residentialshippingcontainerprimer.com

In these steps, the first two can be considered the container selection stage. A single 40-foot (12-meter) container or two 20-foot (6-meter) containers can be used to form a space of same size. It is important that choice of container is done in advance because the structural arrangement can vary depending on the type of container. Steps three to six are the processing stage. Containers are a metal material so welding equipment is needed. In addition, the flammability of insulation materials should also be taken into consideration. Steps seven to eight are the renovation stage. The pipeline should be buried in the middle of the insulation to make the space clean and tidy. Steps ten to twelve are the polishing stage. The bathroom, kitchen, and other facilities should be placed indoors before connecting the building to the pipeline. The remaining decorative materials, such as flooring, walls, and ceiling, can be pasted on the edges of fixed equipment. The final stage is the installation of lamps, switches, and furniture.

2. Research on Container Building Modification

2.1 Container Insulation Measures

Because of its metal structure, which is highly thermal conductive, container insulation is badly needed in order to maintain hospitable indoor thermal environment. Generally speaking, there are three different means for applying container insulation: interior insulation, exterior insulation, and utilizing the built-in cooling abilities of refrigerated containers in the insulation structure. However, due to the difficulty in dismantling and remodifying and their costly price, refridgerated containers tend to be in short supply, making it not the best choice for container building construction. Consequently, interior insulation and exterior insulation are far more common .

2.1.1 Interior Insulation

Applying interior insulation can be completed in a factory. The solid metal exterior of the container and its many perforated holes make hoisting and transportation easily done without damage to the fragile insulation layer.

In applying interior insulation, special attention should be paid on the following areas:

(1) Choose thin insulation materials whenever possible

Due to the limited internal space of the container, it is necessary to guarantee the insulation sufficient to the local climate conditions of the building and carefully calculate the energy-saving performance of different insulation materials. In this case, thin insulation materials should be first taken into consideration in the interests of saving space. For example, filling in the recesses of the container's corrugated metal plating with polyurethane foam insulation makes full use of space. In addition, make use of new highly thermal-resistant insulation materials, such as aerogel and vacuum insulation panels (VIP), to reduce significantly the space occupied by insulation.

(2) Choose the insulation materials that adapt to the environment

Given containers have certain negative physical qualities, such as poor fire resistance and soundproofing, choose insulation materials that help ameliorate these features. For instance, hydrophobic materials are a good choice that can help prevent the container from being corroded from the insulation materials absorbing water.

(3) Choose the insulation materials appropriate to respective sections of the container

Different insulation configurations are needed depending on the part of the container. Insulation of the walls, for example, usually employs a wooden keel-like frame. First, insert the wooden frame in the concave part of the container's corrugated steel plating, then press the wooden frame against the metal baffle and weld the baffle onto the wooden keel. Then, fix the insulation board and external decorative paneling on top of the frame, in accordance with the thickness of the insulation materials. Finally, seal the decorative plating. The use of a wooden frame minimize the occurrence of thermal bridging.

In addition, a steel frame could also be used to fix the insulation and paneling. As shown in figure 30, the Z-shaped frame is spread out every 20 feet (6.1 meters) and welded to the steel structure of the container. The gap between the steel

Figure 30.

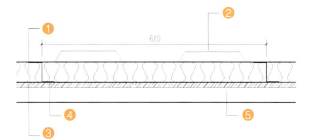

1 Rock wool
2 Steel support set up every other 610 mm
3 Plywood
4 Container shell
5 Fire board

Figure 30. Thermal insulation for wall

Figure 31.

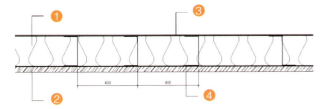

1 Rock wool insulation
2 Use channel steel to fix the 9mm-plywood
3 Container shell
4 Steel trimming beam

Figure 31. Thermal insulation for ceiling

container and decorative paneling is filled with 1.3 feet (0.4meters) of rock wool and covered by .0.3 feet (0.09 meters) of plywood, while a double-layered 0.41 feet (0.125 meters) thick fire-resistant board covers the other side facing the room. The overall thickness of the insulation materials and paneling is 2.46 feet (0.75 meters).

Using a frame to hang decorative paneling is mostly used for the ceiling of the container residence. Primarily insulation materials are chiefly filled in the upper part of the decorative paneling. Overhead illumination in generally embedded in the ceiling surface or fixed in the decorative paneling. As Figure 31 shows, for ceiling insulation, the frame is spaced out every 13.1 feet (4 meters). There is 0.3-foot (0.09-meter) thick plywood fixed under the keel fixed while 3.28-foot (1-meter) thick rock wool insulation material is placed between the plywood and ceiling.

Glued wooden flooring and solid wooden flooring are primarily used in the container residences. To support the indoor furniture and the load generated from residents' activities, the frame on the floor is more densely arranged than the ceiling or walls.

As shown in Figure 32, the flooring is made of 0.92-foot (0.28meters) thick plywood and a steel frame is spaced every 11.8 inches (300 mm). The space between the flooring and the container's metal plating is filled with 3.28 feet (1 meter) of rock wool insulation. Furthermore, the insulation lodged between the steel frame and plywood not reduces thermal bridging, but also improves sound insulation as well.

2.1.2 Exterior Insulation

Exterior thermal insulation is applied to a complete building. In other words, the exterior insulation is usually done after the overall building has been constructed. Preparation of exterior insulation is quite similar that the procedures used for a conventional steel structure. In the construction of the travelodge container hotel, for example, the exterior insulation was once the container was transported and assembled. Because containers are made of metal, the container building would in dire need of shading and insulation during the summer or in hot climates.

2.2.1 Roof Insulation Approaches

Adding onto the roofing structure of the container building is not meant to mitigate rainwater, but to improve shading and ventilation. Generally speaking, based on the structural supports used, there are four types of roofing structure available for insulation: flat, column supporting, pontoon, and external independent structure (Figure 33).

Figure 32.

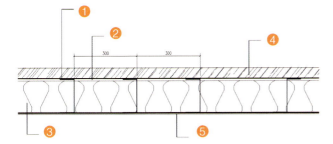

1 Trimming beam set every other 300mm
2 Buffered rubber mat
3 Rock wool insulation material
4 Plywood ground layer
5 Container shell

Figure 32. Thermal insulation for flooring

2.2.2 Wall Shading Approaches

(1). Adding Shading Components to Container

As mentioned earlier, in the container building designed by Meka, bamboo decorative paneling is tightly fixed around the external surface of the metal container and used as a facade decoration. It not only enhances the external appearance of the container building but also plays an important role in shading the metal surface of the container. The same method was also used in the Y Container Experimental Residence designed by Tongji University, who placed dense woven bamboo louvers on the facade to reduce the penetration of sunlight.

(2). Thermal Insulation Coating

The corrugated metal surface of the container itself has its own style and the use of the additional structures in the design will inevitably conceal the unique charm of the container building. Therefore, the use of thermal insulation coating on the external surface of the container is a good way to retain the characteristics of the container facade while still maintaining adequate insulation. According to the performance parameters of Re Dun, a heat-reflective coating developed by Beijing Ryan Kechuang Company, a 200-micron-thick coating from this sort of spray can reflect 92.35% of the thermal energy carried by solar radiation. Additionally, the coating's waterproofing and mildew resistance can help keep the walls dry and prevent the formation of mold. According to data collected by the Vanke Building Research Center, when a material coated with thermal insulation is placed under infrared light, its surface temperature is 12 to 15 degrees Celsius lower than that of a material with an ordinary coating. However, in practice, it will often be necessary to increase the thickness of the insulation coating on the roof and on the south side of the building as circumstances require.

2.2.3 Measures for Container Building Foundation

Due to the prefabricated characteristics of containers, the foundation of the container buildings is different from other types of buildings. However, there are still some similarities between the foundation of container buildings and that of conventional buildings. The foundation in both cases is used to carry the upper structure, to conduct the vertical load, to fix the building's position, prevent the entry of moisture among other roles. On the other hand, the major difference between the two is that the weight of the upper part of the container building is usually much lighter than that of a conventional concrete building. As a result, the foundation is more deeply buried as well as temporary and reusable.

There are several factors that may influence design of the foundation, such as overall state of the area and project, including soil composition, choice of architectural design, climatic factors, and local market preferences. In general, there are three basic types of foundations for container buildings: overhead foundation, concrete plate foundation, and foundation formed from other materials.

(1) Overhead Foundation

The overhead foundation is a very economical foundation that can effectively prevent the build-up of moisture as well as cut down on production time. In addition, it is very convenient to carry out the leveling of the site. Concrete pillars are usually used in small container construction.

Using a cylindrical template after leveling can be a very cheap and quick way to build a foundation that fits the project's needs. Cylindrical concrete columns were used in the previously mentioned projects Bamboo House and Stanko Paul's house to support a water tank. In large buildings, steel structures or concrete pillars are often used as the upper structural support. For example, a large steel column and a raised foundation were used in MVRDV's design of the Amsterdam Cancer Research Center, putting the entire five-story building completely above the wetland surface.

Figure 33.

Name	Illustration	Image
Flat		
Column supporting		
Pontoon		
External independent structure		

Figure 33. Roofing insulation techniques

(2) Concrete Plate Foundation

The overall strength of the concrete plate foundation is more uniform and the settlement is smaller than using the overhead method. The lower concrete floor is affixed to a steel structure, then welded or caulked to the metal container plating after being lifted into place. However, it is particularly worth noting that if the concrete plate base area is large and waterproofing could not be constructed between the container floor and concrete, a drainage system underneath concrete plate foundation should be taken into consideration to prevent water corrosion of the lower part of the container. In the construction of the Keetwonen student dormitory in Amsterdam, The Netherlands, the two ends of the bottom of the containers were fixed onto a metal anchor on the floor and the concrete plates beneath the container slanted inwards to not only facilitate the rapid dispersal of water infiltrating into the lower sections of the container but also created a built-in pipeline under the container.

Other basic forms are reinforced concrete foundations, bar foundations with added masonry structure, and even building foundations built up from tires, timber, and other uncommon building materials.

6.2.4 Procedures in Splicing Together Containers

In many cases, especially for university buildings, it might be necessary to slice the containers in the process of combining them with other container. There are two ways for this slicing: use a welded connection for a permanent connection or us an anchor connection for a temporary connection. Additionally, special treatment is needed for the gap between the containers after the connection has been made to prevent the accumulation rain and dirt through cracks corrosion in the container.

These gaps can be treated in two way. For permanent connections, weld the two containers tightly enough to prevent a gap from forming. For temporary connections or when the gap is too large to be welded, use sealing materials, such as neoprene rubber strips, This type of sealing material is often hydrophobic and aging-resistant. When rubber strips are used for sealing, it is often necessary to make sure that the rubber strip is firmly hammered into the gap to ensure the reliability of the seal. Moreover, the strip should be checked and replaced regularly.

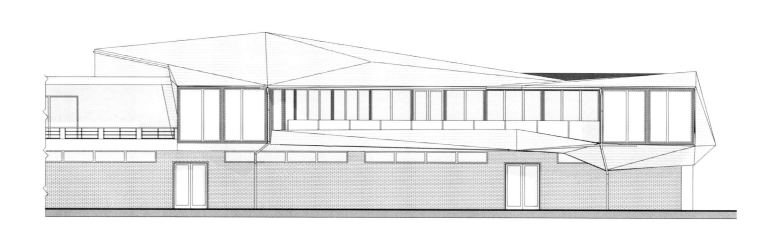

Case Studies

Devil's Corner

Location Sherbourne Road, Apslawn, Tasmania **Area** 6157 square feet (572 square meters) **Completion date** 2015
Design Cumulus Studio **Photography** Tanja Milbourne **Client** Brown Brothers'

01

Visitors winding north along the Tasman Highway on Tasmania's scenic East Coast would be familiar with the Cherry Tree Hill lookout. Few distance away from Cranbrook, over a corridor of eucalypts and scrub, , an iconic granite mountains of the Freycinet Peninsula jutted above Moulting Lagoon jumps into your eyes.

The foreground of the panorama are the lush green blocks of one of Tasmania's largest vineyards, Devil's Corner and its cellar door. Reopened in November 2015, this project for Brown Brothers seeks to simultaneously make safe and amplify the experience of this iconic view to create a new tourism experience on the East Coast of Tasmania. It further promotes the development of relevant industries such as local market and services of providing back drop for seasonal events.

The Cellar Door and Lookout were designed as a loose collection of timber clad buildings. A modern interpretation of traditional farm / rural settlement that gather over time is formed through similar aesthetic and material treatment. The Cellar Door & food market have been collected around a courtyard space which allows shelter and respite from the surrounding environment while allowing views through the tasting space to the Hazards beyond and access to open deck spaces.

Through the careful placement of a series of timber clad shipping containers, visitors are invited to visually explore the landscape within and around the vineyard through curated framed views. The lookout element is a critical component of the design, It is not only a visual signifier for the settlement but also as a way of interpreting the landscape from which the Devil's Corner wines originate. The lookout plays with this idea. The three distinct spaces lead to different and unique views of the site – the SKY, the HORIZON and the TOWER which winds its way upward providing views to each of the compass points before culminating in an elevated and expansive view of the bay.

By creating a dynamic scenic lookout and providing associated facilities, visitors are drawn to a new upgraded cellar door for the Devil's Corner wine label.

The project won the 2016 Tasmanian Architecture Awards: Colin Philp Award for Commercial Architecture and the Colorbond Award for Steel Architecture, and was recognized at the 2016 National Architecture Awards with a National Commendation for Commercial Architecture.

02

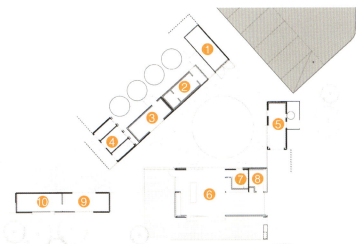

1 Storage container
2 Cold store
3 Retail container 01
4 Existing toilets
5 Retail container 02
6 Tasting & sales
7 Scullery
8 Store
9 Tourism information
10 Private tasting room

Site plan

01 / Front perspective
02 / Rear perspective

Elevations

03-04 / Tombolo Café
05 / The Fishers
06 / Rear perspective

06

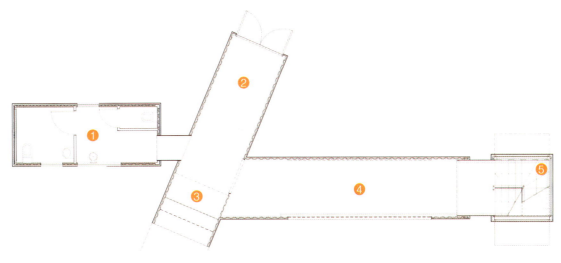

Lookout floor plan

1 Amenities
2 Lookout entrance
3 Sky lookout
4 Horizon lookout
5 Tower lookout

07

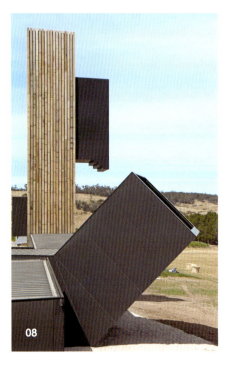

08

07 / Tower view
08 / Angled container by entrance pointing toward sky
09 / Shipping container structure
10-11 / Stairs
12 / Opening with scenic view

Dunraven Container Sports Hall

Location Streatham, London **Area** 12,917 square feet (1200 square meters) **Completion date** 2009
Design Studio Cullinan And Buck Architects Ltd. **Photography** Jun Keung Cheung **Client** London Borough of Lambeth
and Dunraven School

01

Innovative, sustainable and eye-catching, this sports hall designed for Dunraven School in the London Borough of
Lambeth is the first to be built in this way anywhere in the world. Thirty 40' sea containers used as both structure
and internal accommodation create an extremely simple and cost effective building that captures and promotes the
participatory excitement of sports making a multi-purpose community facility that gives the school the best indoor sporting
environment they could wish for, "so much more than a boring shed" whilst staying well within the local authority's strict
budget constraint.

Large areas of glazing, using an immediately recognisable back-garden motif, the domestic greenhouse which
is continued internally with a trowel, a wheelbarrow and watering cans, allow activity in the hall to be seen by
spectators, providing glimpses from the street, connecting the inside action of the building with the outside
life of the surrounding landscape – qualities too often lacking in the ubiquitous and closed box of conventional
sports halls.

Elevations

The orientation of the buildingis carefully considered to maximise its presence on the street, with the north elevation comprising a three-storey arrangement of translucent polycarbonate panels and the clear glazing of the 'greenhouses' cookie-cut on each corner. Along with the internal openings in the first-floor gallery and the clearstory, this positioning of the whole building and its fenestration allows the interior to be flooded with natural daylight without interference from direct sunlight. This daylight and sense of openness also makes the space suitable for exams, assemblies and other important events for the school and the surrounding community.

At night, when the Hall becomes available for community use as a sports facility or a multi-purpose hall, this composition of openings makes the street frontage of the building glow while the lit-up window shapes around the sides further animate the form.

01 / Street frontage
02 / South side
03 / First-floor viewing gallery

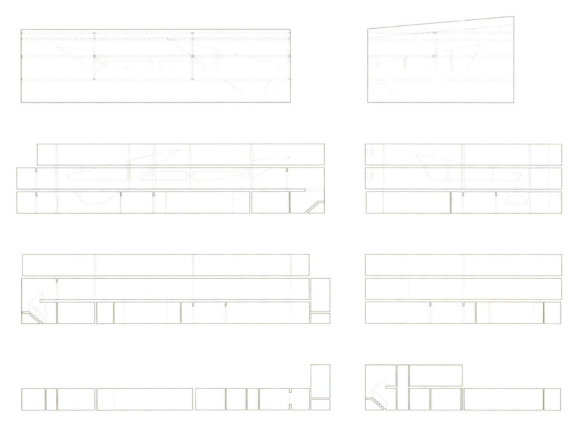

Sections

Commissioned by London Borough of Lambeth and built by Container City (USM) in three months with on-site installation only three days, using funding from the 'Building Schools for the Future' program this innovative approach to building and commitment to sustainability was rewarded by being the 'Best Small Building Project' at the prestigious Building Industry Construction Awards in 2009.This project has led SCABAL to design variations of sea container sports halls in China, Norway, India (under construction), USA and Nigeria.

04 / Inside looking south
05 / Changing rooms
06 / South-east corner and main entrance

Zhao Hua Xi Shi Living Museum

Location Jinshanling of Great Wall, Beijing , China **Area** 26,910 square feet (2500 suqare meters) **Completion date** 2016
Design IAPA Design Consultants **Photography** ZENG Zhe **Client** The Mother Earth Happiness Group

Yin Ma Chuan of the Great Wall – The Seeking the Happiness of Mother Earth Area is a cultural resort built right at the foot of the Great Wall of China. IAPA partnered with SD Great Land Eudemonia Group to design the project, from architecture to landscape, from interior design to construction. The resort blends together environmental protection and art culture. Zhao Hua Xi Shi Living Museum is now complete and in use.

Shipping containers acted as the central material in constructing the Zhao Hua Xi Shi Living Museum. The museum consists of exhibitions, eating areas, lounges, and office spaces all in one. The containers connect to one another by galleries, bridges and platforms, creating a pleasant courtyard environment. The design enhances the natural scenery around the Great Wall, providing fantastic views of the surroundings.

Zhao Hua Xi Shi Living Museum represents the preservation and continuation of traditional Chinese culture. All of the site's various components — the structural form, the indoor and outdoor spaces, the contrast of stone and steel, the timber and hemp, the interaction of corridors, bridges, and viewing platforms — together create a special experience that immerses you in the environment.

01 / Tea room facing observation deck on second floor
02 / Connecting bridge

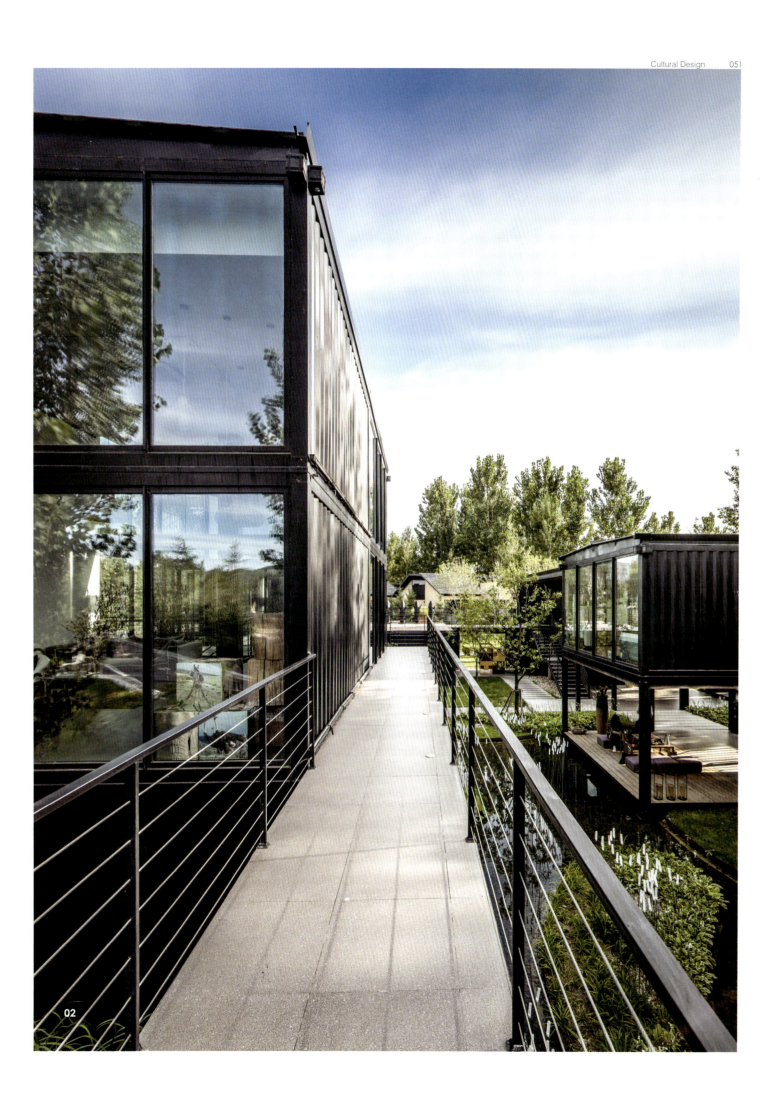

02

03 / Courtyard facing observation tower on the second floor
04 / Courtyard
05 / Kitchen facing courtyard

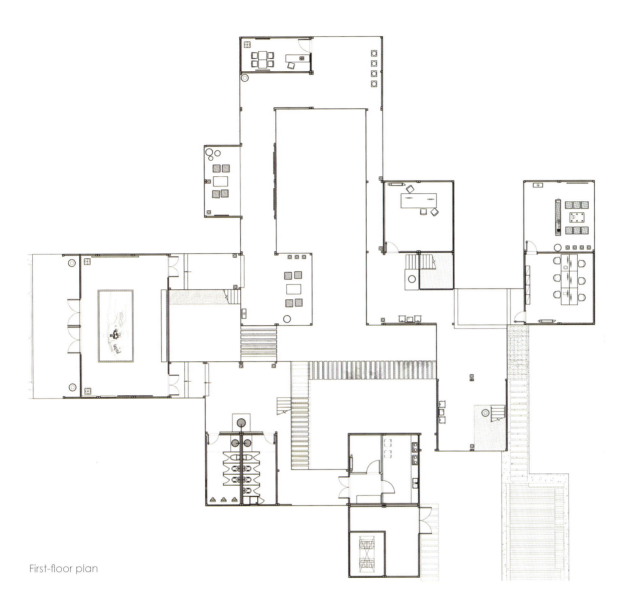

First-floor plan

05

06 / Tearoom
07 / Semi-open tearoom
08 / Walkway

08

KontenerART 2012

Location Warta river, Poznań, Poland **Area** 22819 square feet (2120 square meters) **Completion date:** 2012
Design mode:lina **Photography** Ewa Łowżył, Marcin Ratajczak **Client** KontenerART

01

Tucked away near the Warta River yet still in the center of Poznan, KontenerART is a festival constructed from shipping containers where artists can meet, relax, and collaborate together in workshops and exhibitions. Until the end of August, spare containers are available for individual artists, who use them as studios. In 2012, KontenerART held over 35 concerts, 60 workshops, and film screenings.

The architectural team mode:lina packed an lively cultural experience in their design for the festival space, filled with wooden palettes, hammocks and beach chairs, right in sync with the summer mood and creates an atmosphere open to everyone.

Containers were the perfect choice of material, given they are practical in addition to having their own aesthetic value. Their mobility and low cost made setting up the festival space a simple process, even with a limited budget.

The bar counters were built from cheap OSB board, showing how a great visual effect can be made at little expense. As for the containers themselves, those used from music gigs and other events had their walls replaced with glass panels, making them completely transparent. That way, visitors can watch the events from wherever they are in festival space. Other containers were left unaltered, functioning as much-needed storage spaces. Acting as warehouses, these containers ensured valuable items and equipment was protected from the elements and from theft.

With containers all modified in different fashions, mode:lina has put together their own mini-community right in Poznan, all thanks to the modest shipping container.

01 / Containers with bar and dancefloor
02 / View of Warta River and Pazanan cathedral from container roof

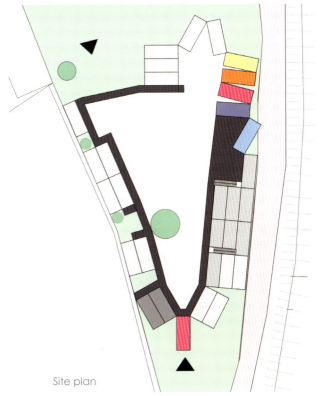

Site plan

03

04

03 / Logotypes of project partner
04-05 / Multifunctional terrace for workshops and relaxation

APAP OPEN SCHOOL

Location Anyang, South Korea **Area** 5500 square feet (511 square meters) **Completion date** 2010 **Design** LOT-EK, Ada Tolla + Giuseppe Lignano, Principals, Tommy Manuel, Project **Photography** Kim Myoung-sik **Client** Kyong Park, Artistic Director of APAP2010, Anyang Public Art

01 / View from river
02-03 / View from pedestrian walkway

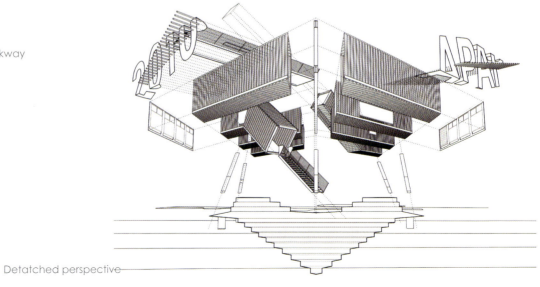

Detatched perspective

To give the OpenSchool a space to conduct their public arts program, the team designed a shipping container structure along the river's edge to act as a recreational center for visitors, spectators, and actors.

Eight shipping containers are skewed to a 45-degree angle and combined in a fishbone pattern, culminating in a large arrow-like structure hovering three meters over the landscape. The structure is strategically placed over a pedestrian walkway in Hakwoon Park right on the edge of a drop to the river bank, marking the location as a focal point of gathering, resting and spectating.

Three different and interconnected areas provide a sequence of varied spatial experiences within the OpenSchool. At ground level, taking advantage of the existing sloping topography, the footprint of the shipping container structure becomes a public amphitheater. The lower section of the amphitheater offers a viewpoint on the landscape along the river edge, while the upper section, reaching a higher level, engages the main open space below the OpenSchool structure, transforming it into a space for performances. The social spaces entice public gathering and community exchange. A shipping container, directly connected to the pedestrian paths, invites access to the upper levels.

02

03

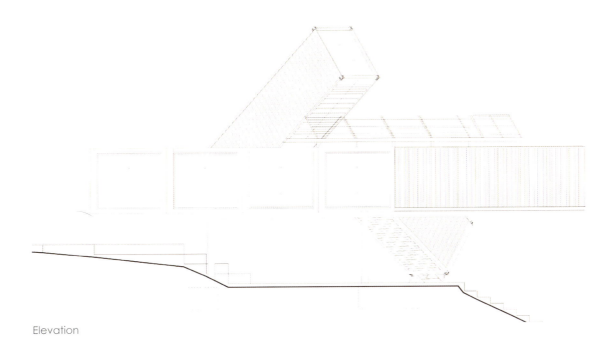

Elevation

At the second level, carved out of the hovering containers' interior space, the area includes two studios for artists-in-residence, as well as one large, open, multi-purpose space that functions as a meeting/assembly room and exhibition space.

The two frontal walls along the northwest axis and at the structure's most dramatic overhang of, are solid and pierced only by a series of peep-holes. Located at different heights to be accessible for kids and adults, the tubes frame different views within the surrounding landscape, focusing on natural and urban snapshots of the neighborhood. The containers' short sides are entirely glazed allowing natural light, cross ventilation, and views to the park path below.

03 / Rear view with structural truss
04 / Entrance
05 / Exhibition space with peep-holes toward surrounding landscape
06 / Exhibition/event space

A stairway, contained within a shipping container, directs to the structure top level. A long deck area, at the third level, stretches over the river. Resembling a diving board, the roof deck offers an amazing view from its suspended position while two long benches provide a space for social interaction.

The dramatic visual treatment of the new structure for the APAP OpenSchool, with its bright yellow and black colors, it is as visible as a landmark for cars and passersby within the urban fabric of Anyang.

07

07 / Stair to outdoor deck
08 / Exit to outdoor deck

Hai d3

Location Dubai, United Arab Emirates **Area** 20204 square feet (1877 square meters) **Completion date** 2015
Design ibda design **Photography** Sadao Hotta

Hai d3 is a mixed-use community that serves as headquarters to the Dubai Design District, the hub for emerging local creative talent in the UAE. With the need for a temporary facility to host community projects and events, it was crucial for Hai d3 to be flexible and able to be quickly assembled and disassembled in a sustainable manner. Integrating traditional Arabic neighborhood planning into the design, the architecture was composed as a modular system, using 40-foot (12-meter) shipping containers in a stacking and layout arrangement.

The shipping containers offered a building element that well suited the history of the city, given that Dubai is a port city with an urban fabric of transience and change. The containers were considered as items that have traveled all over the world, each carrying a history with energy embedded within them. Ultimately, they were collected together into this single project to converse amongst each other, serving as the background for a contemporary Arabic neighborhood. The project offers a contemporary fiction of the historical Middle Eastern city, reinterpreting the expansion and contraction of its pathways as well as being defined by its vibrant, public spaces. By using a recycled, mass-produced product, the project intentionally preserves the raw and the industrial form of the containers while re-imagining the modern Arabic urban fabric as well.

Seventy-five containers are arranged in Hai d3, with six different stacking layouts according to programmatic use: workshop, library, cafe, art galleries, prayer rooms and retail spaces. Key to the project is the configuration of outdoor "pockets" of space, serving as courtyards for each building. Both the courtyards and landscape arrangements complement the industrial language of the architecture promote activity within the naturally lit spaces, and offer

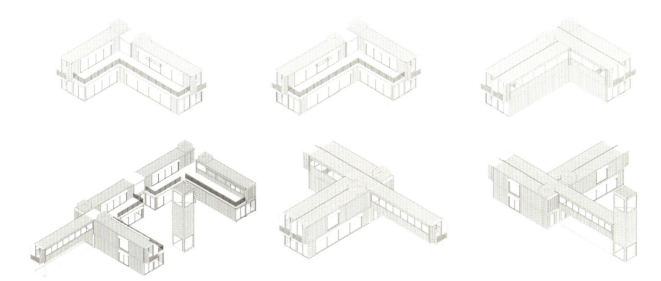

Various arrangements of containers according to functional needs

a motivating and productive atmosphere. Full-height windows were punctured into the shipping containers and integrated into the building interiors so that people can better enjoy the outdoor landscape and views of the Dubai skyline. Additionally, these transparencies define a connection between the inside and outside, making the spaces flexible for both summer and winter temperatures.

The climate of the Middle East played a decisive role in the project. The sunlight and necessary methods for temperature control had to be taken into consideration. Passive cooling of the courtyard and landscape spaces occurs with containers acting as "wind towers," strategically placed across the site. These wind towers distribute natural ventilation by catching high draft winds and funneling them towards the courtyards within the community. This modern spin on a traditional ventilation strategy provides an efficient and eco-friendly method of cooling the Hai d3 outdoor areas, making them an inviting space for a revitalizing walk, creative mingling, and curated events. Additional program and aesthetic elements were implemented with 20-foot (6-meter) service containers. One of these extra containers acts as an entrance piece, welcoming people to the district and serving as a multi-functional venue for artists to host movie screenings, gatherings, and outdoor workshops.

The Hai d3 community uses flexible, modular forms in traditional Arabic arrangements, offering its users a platform for creative productivity. Once gathered, visitors can embrace the dynamism of their work, and in turn, use Hai d3 as a foundation for propelling the creative industry of the Middle East.

01 / Repurposed shipping containers as 'wind towers'
02 / View of courtyard from residence
03 / Courtyard

04 / Benches designed as part of landscape
05 / Courtyard and communal gathering space
06 / Glass frame directly connecting with exterior
07 / Glass usage ensuring abundance of natural light

Seoul Youth Zone

Location Seoul, South Korea **Completion date** 2015 **Design** Kangsoo Lee, Joohyung Kang, Jinyoung Oh, Taekho Lee
Photography Seungbin Bae and Kangsoo Lee

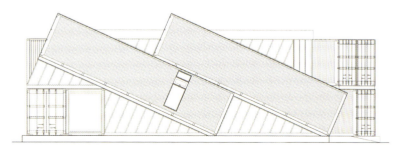 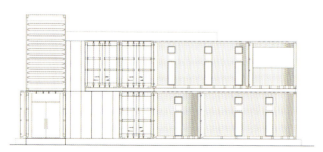

Elevations

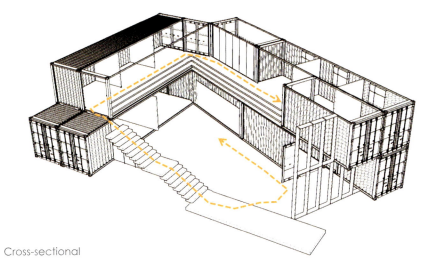

Cross-sectional

The Seoul Youth Zone in Daebang-dong is an architectural facility composed of 13 containers, providing space for collaborative youth activities, while still being environmentally sustainable and flexible in form. The youth and young adults of Korea have faced an era that continues to discourage them in job seeking, marriage, housing, and social relationships. It seems evident that the society should take their struggles seriously and begin to look for ways to help the young adult generation. As a solution for the social problems, the city of Seoul has planned a place that is open to young adults and provides them diverse activities and services, including business-related. The space, Seoul Youth Zone, will enable the stressed youth to let go burdens weighing them down and enter a zone of zero gravity, hence the name. It is a space where the youth can both experience rich vibrant culture and network with each other. Seoul Youth Zone in Daebang-dong is the cornerstone for such cultural activity spaces in Seoul. It is meant to act as a platform for groups and individuals to express themselves as well as share their culture with one another.

01-02 / Side view

Seoul Youth Zone is located in a public parking area next to a vegetable farm by Daebang subway station. Given the limited time and finances available to develop the entire site, freight containers were no doubt the best choice. The building takes advantage of the containers' materials, presenting an energetic and daring appearance that captures the spirit of youth. The triangular corner of the site and existing pedestrian paths dictated the orientation of the building layout. The series of containers wrap around, creating perimeter structure and forming space and a atrium lounge for events and various other activities. The interior space consists of seminar rooms, communal kitchens, restrooms, and office spaces. The floor plan of the building was carefully considered for optimizing efficiency. Rooms needing special equipment, such as utilities, are clustered into one container while two containers are combined to a single section to hold office and seminar rooms.

As one proceeds from the entrance to the interior spaces, one first encounters the atrium, the seminar area, and the open kitchen. The seminar rooms themselves can be expanded into the atrium. These open areas create an environment conducive to relaxing, learning, and cultural exchange.
Two slanted containers create spaces for staircases and exhibitions. The height of the staircases symbolizes freedom, soaring over one's problems while in the Seoul Youth Zone. The large width of the staircases invites young adults to rest and socialize comfortably. The gap between the two leaning containers is utilized as a mini-lounge that receives abundant natural light. The second floor has six office spaces all connected through an interior balcony that enables one to look down at the first floor atrium. These offices are inhabited by various entrepreneurs. A closed office space is provided for the management of the building.

03-06/ Interior view

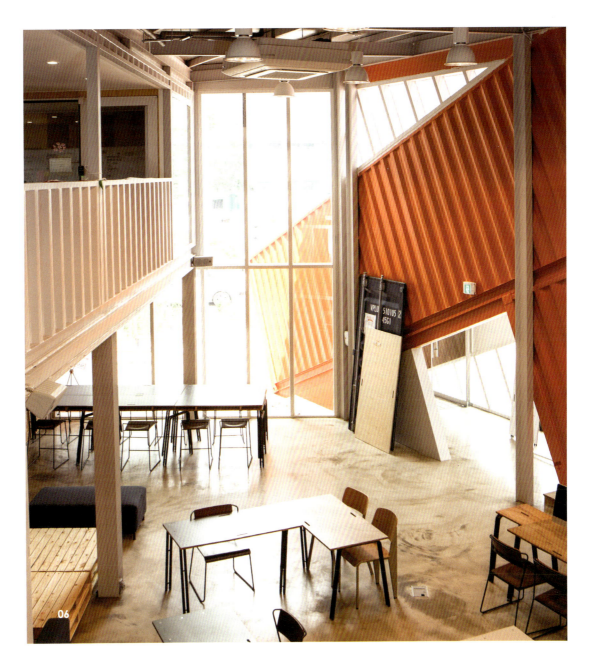

06

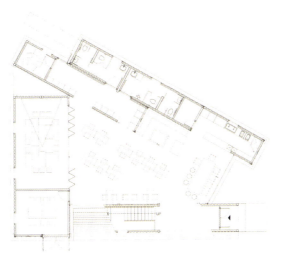

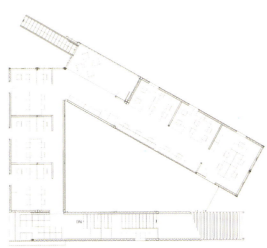

Plan

Taitung Aboriginal Galleria

Location Taitung, Taiwan China **Area** 20,677 square feet(1,921 square meters) **Completion date** 2016
Design Bio-Architecture Formosana **Photography** Lucas K. Doolan **Client** Taitung County Government

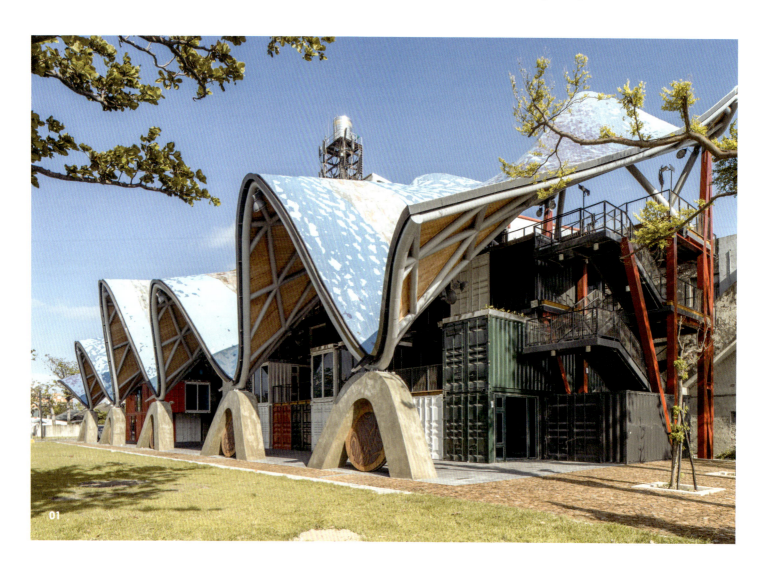

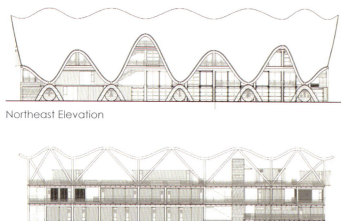

Northeast Elevation

Southwest Elevation

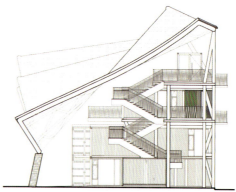

Southeast Elevation

Taiwan not only is the origin place of Austronesian culture, it is also located at the northern-most area of the cultural region. Taitung, covering just 164,042 feet (50,000 meters) has a rich topography, ranging from beaches to mountains. Throughout this wide variety of environments, Taitung is home to seven different tribes. Austronesian architectural has been deeply shaped by the local climate. Ocean, forests — all parts of nature play an important role in this architectural style. This relationship with nature profoundly influenced us in designing a gallery for Austronesian artwork.

This project aims to capture the architectural essence of Austronesian culture. The design uses a large roof covering, creating a shaded space suitable for Austronesian activities. The design facilitates wind flow throughout the structure and allows sunlight to shine through the beetle nut trees, ferns, shell flowers, and various other types of Austronesian plant life, creating an experience of being in the midst of a rainforest.

Aboriginal handcraft shops made from recycled container houses are scattered throughout the space to create a marketplace atmosphere. In Taiwan, approximately 10000 containers are retrieved from the ocean each year, providing about 161,459 square feet (15,000 square meters) of recycled space. Unlike conventional buildings, this project consists of two different types of spaces: individually air conditioned units and naturally ventilated outdoor walkways. In Taitung's tropical climate, air conditioning in separate units reduces cooling demands by 50% and the electricity use by 60%.

The curved shape of the roof represents the changing topography of Taitung. The slanted surface collects rainwater into five small ponds at the plaza. Aboriginal art often utilizes talismans to convey historical or spiritual stories. The steel structure on the roof incorporates diamond shapes to symbolize the eyes of ancestral spirits.

Conceptual Sketch

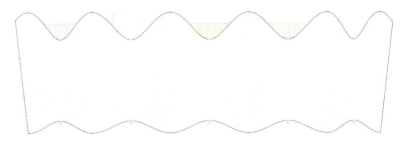

Roof Plan

01 / Exterior of Taitung Aboriginal Galleria
02 / Curved roof to collect rainwater
03 / Containers stacked up in different directions

04

04 / Roofed semi-outdoor space
05 / Staircase
06 / Wide platforms connecting different shops
07 / Open space between shops

05

06

07

OceanScope

Location Incheon, South Korea **Area** 3767 square feet (350 square meters) **Completion date** 2010 **Design** AnL Studio (Keehyun Ahn and Minsoo Lee), ZZangPD (Chang Gil-Hwang) Architecture+Interior Designers **Photography** AnL Studio. **Client** Incheon Metropolitan City, South Korea

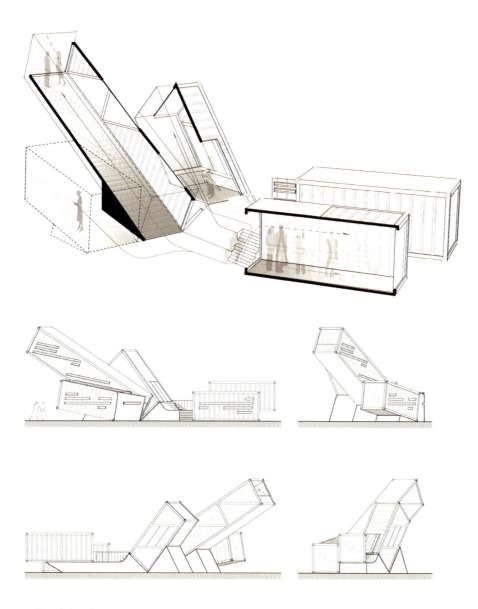

Cross-sectional drawing

01

01/Front perspective

OceanScope was an initiative from the Mayor of Incheon City, which has one of the biggest ports in South Korea. For the project, Architecture+Interior Designers and AnL Studio (Keehyun Ahn and Minsoo Lee) together designed a public observatory deck in Incheon, made entirely of recycled materials, used freight containers in particular.

Used containers have frequently been repurposed as temporary shelter, due to being relatively inexpensive, yet indiscriminate use of the containers has resulted in structures that clash with the natural environment, creating issues in rural parts of South Korea.

The designers kept this problem in mind while working on the project. OceanScope aimed to harness the potential of containers in being practically reused for public space as well as to provide the bleak containers with new functional aesthetics that can be assimilated within rural landscapes.

02

Oceanscope consists of five recycled containers, forming an observatory deck with three containers and a space for temporary exhibits with the remaining two. Instead stacking the containers in a conventional fashion, AnL Studio envisioned an architectural landmark embodying various features and functions, ranging from framing scenic views to conveying the connotations of daringness and freedom associated with the city.

In accomplishing this goal, OceanScope is located in an area of Incheon famed for its sunsets. The project uses sustainable designs to allow people to better appreciate such natural beauty. Because the building site's elevation was too low to properly view the sunsets, tilted at various angles (10', 30', 50'). This allows people to ascend the structure and watch the sunset at different points as well as see other nearby sites, such as the ocean and New Incheon Bridge.

02 / Side view
03-04 / Details

03

06

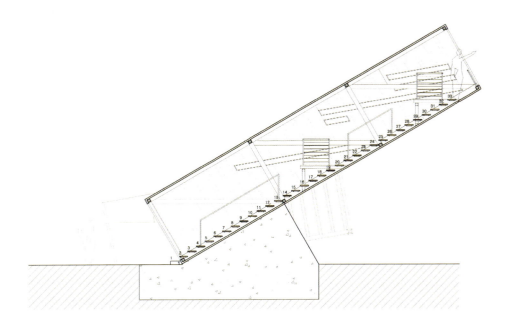

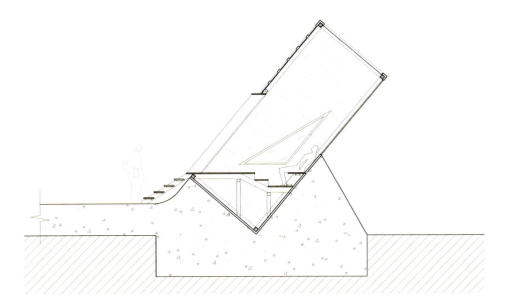

Sections

Nomadic Museum

Location Pier 54, New York, NY, USA **Area** 60,000 square feet (5574 square meters) **Completion date** 2006
Design Shigeru Ban Architects **Photography** Michael Moran

01

Nomadic Museum was planned as an organized system for transporting a museum moving from one city to another, but putting this into practice proved to be unexpectedly quite difficult.

In March of 2005, the 45,208 square feet (4200 square meters) Nomadic Museum was built in New York on Pier 54, reaching out into the Hudson River. It attracted 300,000 visitors during a run of three months then, as scheduled, was moved to the next site in January of 2006 at the parking lot adjacent to Santa Monica Pier, this time expanded to 55,972 square feet (5200 square meters).

As the main structure of the museum consists of 20-feet (6-meter) long shipping containers, which are rented locally at each location, only a small part of the construction materials need to be transported, such as the tensile roof membrane and the supporting structure of 24.6-foot (7.5-meter) diameter paper tube columns and 9.8-foot (3-meter) diameter paper tube trussed roof sections. The logistical transportation of materials was easy, but in Santa Monica, two new unexpected issues had to be overcome.

Firstly, the floor area had to be increased by 10,763 square feet (1000square meters) in order for a bookstore and several cinemas of varying sizes to show new films taken by Gregory Colbert. The 673-foot (205-meter) long and only 65.6-foot (20 meters) wide linear gallery on the pier in New York was altered to a 541 x 492 feet (165 x 150 meters) semi-square shape to fit Santa Monica's completely different site conditions. Therefore, the gallery was split up into two halves aligned in parallel with space in the center for the bookstore and the movie theaters. As in New York, the containers were stacked in the same checkerboard pattern and secured at the corners utilizing the container's existing system of joints.

The second problem the design team had to face was different regulations between states. In New York, the Nomadic Museum had been approved as temporary building, allowing for a simple foundation by placing H-beams under the containers. The different regulations in Santa Monica made approval as a temporary building impossible. Furthermore, the structure was required to be able to withstand 26 kN of force (beneath the container at each span), double the earthquake resistance standards of what is usually required, which led to installing anchored foundations.

After the exhibition in Santa Monica, the Nomadic Museum traveled to Tokyo among other Asian cities and afterwards to Europe. Through the experiences in New York and Santa Monica, Shigeru Ban realized that the difficulty with traveling museums is the gap between authorities' preconceptions and the artist's unbounded creative urges.

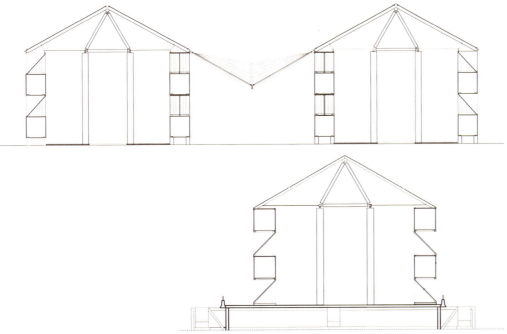

Cross-sections

01-02 / Nomadic Museum-LA

03

03-04 / Nomadic Museum-LA

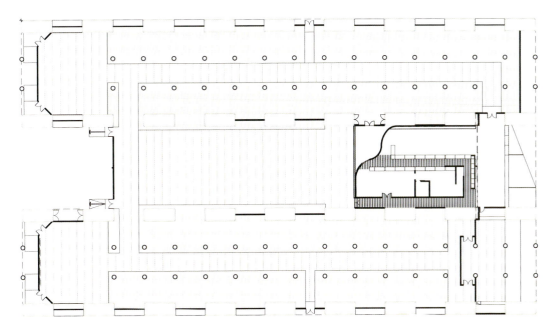

Plan

Jazzboksen 2016

Location Kongsberg, Norway **Area** 1550 square feet (144 square meters) **Completion date** 2016
Design mmw arkitekter as one **Photography** © mmw.no > Nils Petter Dale, © mmw.no > Tommy Johansen
Kongsberg Jazzfestival 2016

01

The Kongsberg Jazz Festival aspires to be an open and inclusive festival, suitable for grown-ups as well as children. This is one of Norway's oldest jazz festivals and attracts approximately 30,000 visitors to Kongsberg every year. The program profile focuses on new and innovative jazz and aims to deliver the country's most exciting jazz program.

The team built five new containers placed in the center of Kongsberg as part of the jazz festival. The containers are meant to stimulate social interaction during the music festival. Here, people can come and enjoy the music while enjoying each other's company. After a successful jazz festival with our pilot project "Magasinet," the team rebuilt the container structure the year after, in 2016, but changed the name to "The Jazzbox."

The Jazzbox consists of five 40-foot (12 meters) containers, making the construction mobile. The open construction allows for very easy access both in and out. A large sail is stretched over the scene and attached to the two highest containers to shelter from rain. The audience can either be seated under the roof and listen to the concert up close or sit outside where they can enjoy the music in the sun. Using containers for the design was a wonderful choice. They have a cool sheen perfect for the atmosphere of the jazz festival.

01 / Entrance
02 / Top-down rendering

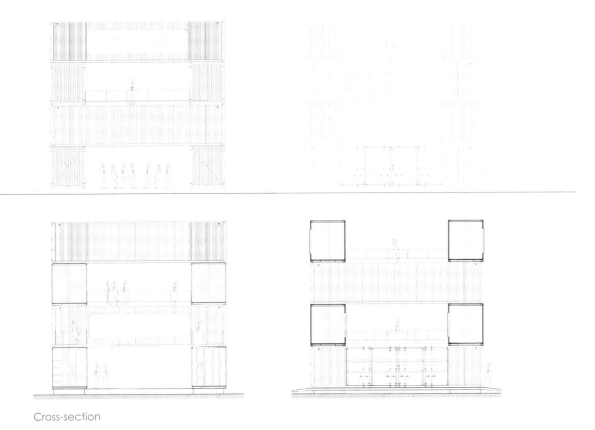

Cross-section

02

Plan

03 / Stage interior
04 / Entrance to Jazz Box

03

04

Marche in the Forest

Location Inuyama, Japan **Area** 1507 square feet (140 square meters) **Completion date** 2016
Design Hiroaki Kajiura Environment Architecture Design Office Hiroaki Kajiura **Photography** Teruro Yoshiike
Client Katsumi Sahashi

01

01 / Pocket park shops surrounded by container shop

The castle town in the middle of Inuyama Castle is a national treasure of Japan. Unfortunately, a fire in 2015 destroyed many of the historical buildings and the area required serious reconstruction. For the project, the team designed a pocket park in a commercial area using seven shipping containers. The designers hoped their project in helping to revitalize the castle town, not only reopens the area up to tourists, but has appeal to locals as well.

Because the land is on a 20-year lease, the designers thought about using containers for environmental and economic reasons. Given castle town is a long narrow area, the designers decided to develop new open space adjacent to the castle town and designed a park there. In the area, containers were all used as stores and restrooms, all facing a public. In the center of the square is a well, which serves two purposes. First, the designers felt water had an important symbolic meaning, considering much of the area had previously been destroyed due to a fire. Second, the well serves a practical use, providing water to the rest of the plaza.

Nature is highly interconnected. A forest must be protected in order to protect the rest of the environment. If forests becomes destroyed or polluted, this will impact the nearby plains and waters as well. As such, the design also placed special consideration on integrating with the natural environment. Each container is covered different type of wood, all locally sourced. The uneven wooden exterior gives both a visual and tactile experience, especially since the wood on each container has each been carved with its own design, yet still distinctly Japanese..

With this design, the team hoped to rekindle an aspect of Japanese culture in the process of revitalizing this area. Sitting on the roof deck overlooking the plaza, one can sense the nature, history, and culture of Inuyama.

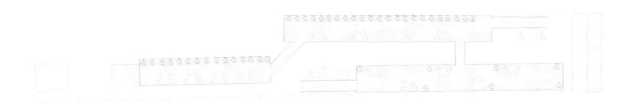

Rooftop plan

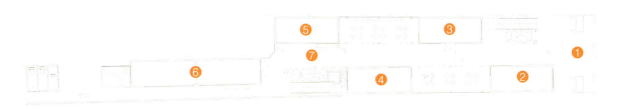

First-floor plan

1 Gate
2 Shop 1
3 Shop 2
4 Shop 3
5 Shop 4
6 Shop 5
7 Pocket park

Elevation

02 / Containers decorated with tree placement
03 / Tables and chairs on container roof overlooking city
04 / Shop interior

04

Conteneur Bell

Location Québec, Canada **Area** 2176 square feet (202 square meters) **Completion date** 2014
Design Hatem+D **Photography** Loki Box Design

Hatem + D Architecture was asked by the Loki Box Design Team to submit a design of a pavilion for the Bell Company, sponsor of several cultural events. It was important to design a facility that could be conveniently transported across the country to the heart of the festivals and the spectacular events.

This jaw-dropping, award-winning design harnesses the power of space and light to create an irresistible pull perfect for even the world's most prestigious events. Our multiple award-winning flagship array is a breathtaking example of modular design and ease of mobility. Customizable for any brand, the design consists of six containers soaring 36 feet (11 meters) high, a total of 2176 square feet (663 meters) of useable space spanning four levels, a giant exterior screen, multiple interior LED screens, a VIP rooftop deck, HVAC, and much, much more.

The project was intended to provide videos and pictures, such as shows, interviews and presentations of products and services offered by Bell. The project therefore works as a cultural and commercial hub, people coming to gather together.

01 / Front view
02 / Side view

02

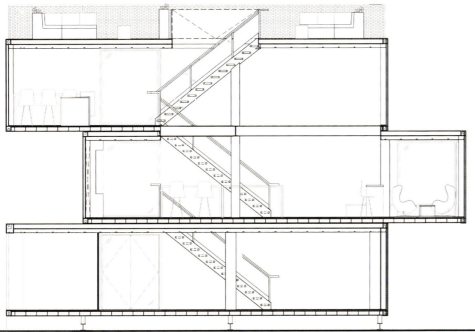

Elevation

03-05 / Interior view

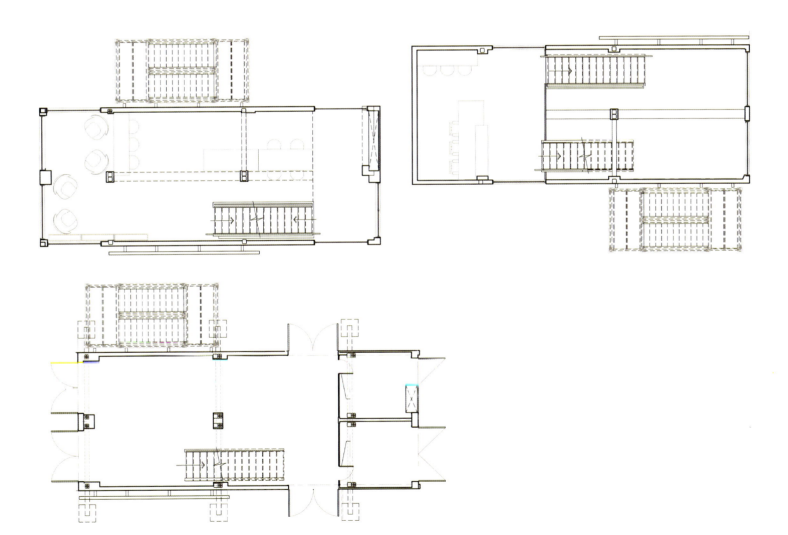

Plans

So Table Kobe0330

Location Kobe , Japan **Area** 1966 ft2 (182.64 m2) **Completion date:** 2017 **Design** A.S.A.P.designlab, Katsuyoshi Shindoh,Dalian GEKEA Modular Thechnology Co.,Ltd **Photography** Loki box Design

Given its prime geographical location facing the mountain and sea, Kobe Port has been a center of economic development and cultural exchange since ancient times. Now, Kobe Port has developed into an international trading port.

So Table Kobe 0330 is an Italian restaurant located in the Meriken Park, which is in the heart of Kobe Port. The Meriken Park attracts a large number of young tourists from Japan and overseas every day. Because of its close proximity to Kobe Port Tower,the Meriken Park, together with the Kobe Tower, are considered symbols of Kobe.

When designing So Table Kobe 0330, the designers adopted the architectural design of the cargo containers, as Kobe Port is a major logistics base for international ports. People can feel Kobe's authentic nature, history, food culture, and way of life through this building. This was the fundamental goal in designing the project.

The architectural design consists of two sections, 40 feet and 20 feet, which take full advantage of the containers' precise dimensions. The visual appearance produces tension and rhythm throughout the building by sliding the second layer of the 40-foot section to the outside about 4 feet (1.2 meters). In addition, thanks to this sliding and the resulting overflow space, the pressure brought by the low ceiling, which is in the inherent nature of containers, is eliminated. A 13-foot (4-meter) glass window was set in the central ventilation space to provide the interior with abundant external light. A roof deck is set on top of the building so that people can enter from the upper part of the building as well as enjoy the night view of Kobe Port from the roof.

The name of the project, So Table Kobe 0330, comes from Japan's primary international calling code, KOBE 0330. The project itself symbolizes a port open both to the domestic audience and to foreign countries. Stakeholders hope that "So Table Kobe 0330", together with Kobe Port, can become a new symbol of Kobe's charm in the future.

01 / Front view
02 / Side view

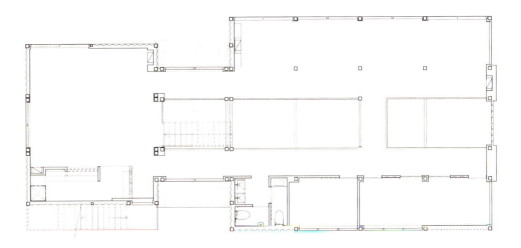

1 Restaurant
2 Entrance
3 Office
4 Kitchen

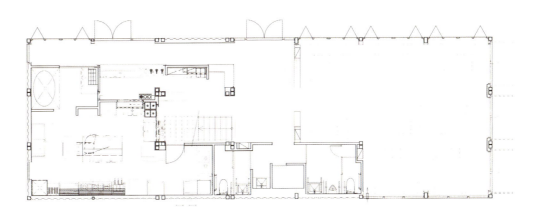

04

03 / Restaurant area on the second floor
04 / Roof deck area

ContainHotel

Location Czech Republic **Area** 646 square feet (60 square meters) **Completion date:** 2015 **Design** ARTIKUL architects - Ing. arch. Pavel Lejdar, Ing. arch. Jan Gabriel, Ing. arch. Jakub Vlcek **Photography** Michal Hurych

01 / Front perspective
02 / Rear perspective

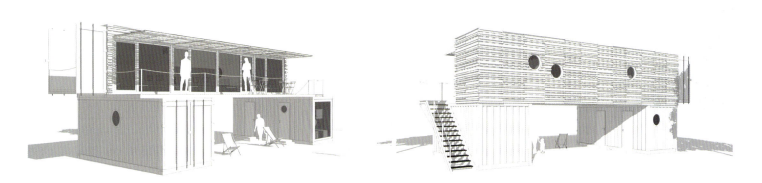

Perspectives

The architects at ARTIKUL were tasked with designing a small hotel for a campsite by the Elbe River near the town of Litoměřice in the Czech Republic. The hotel was to be environmentally friendly and self-sufficient while also being mobile, allowing for easy disassembly, and adaptable to the changing seasons. Furthermore, the architects had to create this hotel using just three shipping containers.

After four months, the architects completed a five-room hotel with two 20-feet (6 meter) containers and one 40-feet (12 meter) container on top. Downstairs consists of sanitary facilities, a storeroom, a tech room, and a four-bed guest room. Upstairs has four additional rooms, each with a fantastic view of the river and surrounding hills, and a shared terrace. Despite each room only having one glazed wall, the space still has good ventilation and blends in well with the overall scenery.

Birch plywood is important material in the design, forming the ceiling and walls as well as all the custom-made furniture. Different shades of linoleum differentiate the rooms, accented with industrial lightning and other decorations.

The minimalism both in design and choice of materials highlight the central themes of the hotel: beach atmosphere with maritime aesthetics and a modern nomad vibe. Using dark-blue container in its original color as well as the round windows and railings made of nets and rope further enhances these themes.

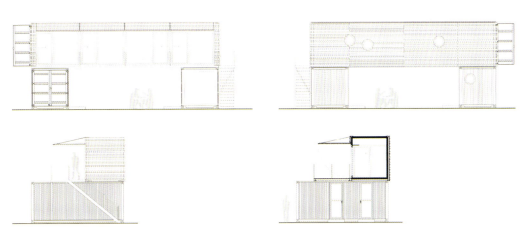

Elevations

The containers are placed on railroad sleepers. They function separately and autonomously, connected only to a local electric power source. The container with the public facilities has a built-in water reservoir to supply showers and sinks, which are equipped with water-saving taps. Also, the bathrooms are equipped with modern waterless toilets. Only biodegradable decorations are used for the hotel. For example, to avoid intense heat in the rooms during summer, an awning is attached above the glazed walls with facades made of waste wood planks from a nearby sawmill, acting as sun breakers.

03 / Interior of double room with common terrace
04 / Common terrace
05 / Double room with balcony
06 / Detail of double room with balcony

Second-floor plan

07 / Interior of four-bed room
08 / Window of four-bed room

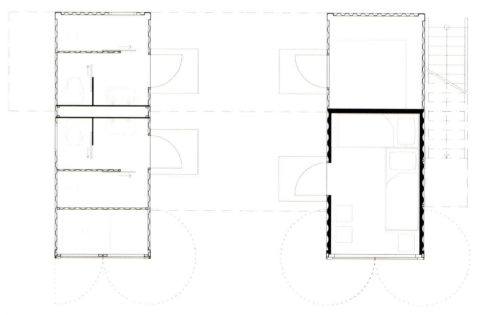

First-floor plan

Container Stack Pavilion

Location Dongshan, China **Area** 3308 square feet (307.3 square meters) **Completion date** 2015
Design People's Architecture Office(He Zhe, James Shen, Zang Feng)
Photography People's Architecture Office **Client** Eastern Heights Real Estate Co. Ltd.

01-04 / Exterior

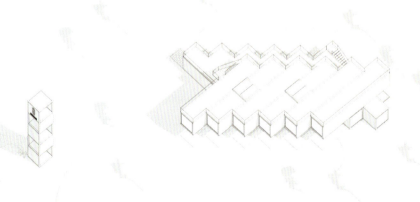

Top-down sketch

Container Stack Pavilion is a small display space, refurbished from freight containers. It can be reused after exhibitions or disassembled and relocated as a decentralized service facility. Through techniques, such as stacking, stretching, and staggering, simple rectangular structures can be combined into a variety of spaces with different functions. Twelve containers of equal length are divided into two groups. The six containers in each group are placed backwards one by one and arranged in zigzag pattern. The upper and lower groups are vertically arranged in a row so that a cantilevered structure can be formed on one end with a sandpit below, which can be used as place for children to play. A terrace on the second floor creates space for outdoor activities and connects with container terrace on the third floor by a staircase. In the room, the roof and floor of the overlapping parts of the two layers are removed, so that the upper and lower two layers of space are connected to form an atrium.

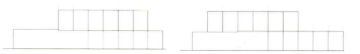

Elevation 1   Elevation 2

05

Natural Light enters from the top via skylights. Overhead bars with lighting embedded lighting are placed in the same direction as the container in order for the light from the upper sections easily reaches the ground floor. Each container is assembled separately and the large transparent glass windows on either side break the sense of confinement often associated with containers. The containers themselves have been painted yellow and red, which makes them stand out most strikingly against the city's grey background. Adjacent to the highway, Container Stack Pavilion reaches out in different directions with its windows, showing off all the direction areas of the city.

06

05-07 / Interior
08 / Exterior

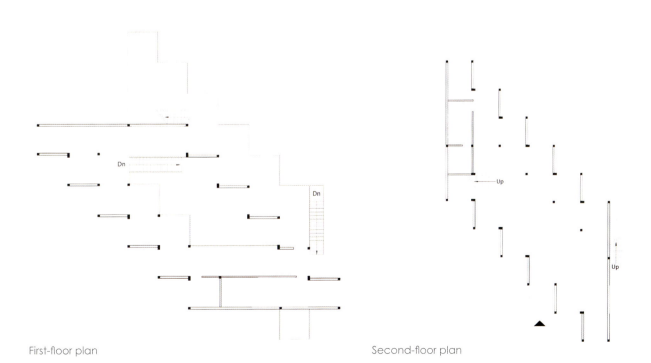

First-floor plan   Second-floor plan

Ccasa Hostel

Location Vietnam **Area** 2099 square feet (195 square meters) **Completion date** 2016
Design Ngo Tuan Anh **Photography** Quang Tran

01

01 / Entrance
02 / Rendering

Ccasa Hostel is the first hostel in Nha trang, Vietnam built entirely from shipping containers. The hotel is located north of the city, about three kilometers from the city center and three minutes' walk from the beach.

The hostel was designed for backpackers following a central idea that everyone who stays will feel connected, like one big family. Ccasa has all the amenities of a family home: shared kitchen area, washing area with toilets and bathrooms, cabin beds, living room, and a terrace on the roof as a recreational area. Consequently, the rooms themselves were compacted to provide the bare minimum space needed for space. Conversely, the communal area was expanded to encourage social interaction among the guests.

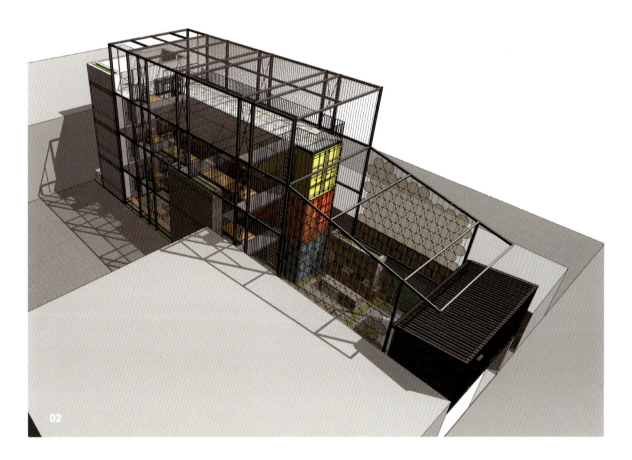

02

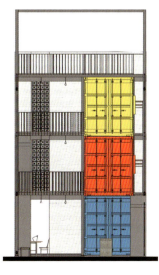

Front elevation   Section 1   Section 2

Ccasa Hostel feels durable and industrial, with the use of steel frames and shipping containers. Yet, the hostel also seems in harmony with nature, given the plentiful greenery and the pergola, which not only adds even more plants to the area, but also provides shade and keeps visitors in the hostel cool. Moreover, the hostel references themes in old Vietnamese architecture through the use of flat winnowing baskets, old wood windows, and rustic cement.

03 / Common space

The hostel is divided into three separate sections: the serving area, the washing area, and the sleeping area. The serving area primarily consists of black metal sheets and steel frames. The washing area, on the other hand, was constructed simply, using just concrete bricks painted white. The sleeping area is made up of three old shipping containers, each one painted one of the primary colors to symbolize the different types of bedrooms. The three sections connect to a large common area, allowing ease of mobility between the different sections. As a result, the project feels harmoniously put together.

Another notable aspect of the project is the entrances to the bedrooms. Instead of cramped hallways, the designers installed open-air bridges covered with plants, making entering or leaving the sleeping section a pleasant experience for any guest. Moreover, the designers made the daring move of stretching hammocks over gaps in the bridges, allowing guests to feel like they are floating in the midst of nature.

Since the renovation, Ccasa Hostel has become a trendy destination for travelers. Furthermore, the new design helps reduce the building's carbon footprint and overall environmental impact to the city.

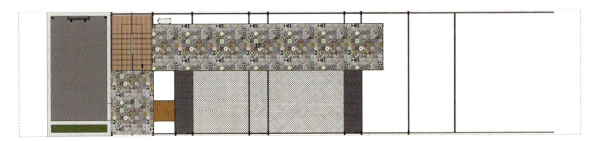

Top floor

Third floor

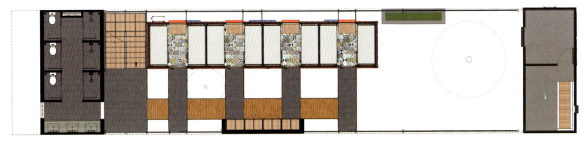

Second floor

First floor

04 / Detail
05 / Top-down view
06 / Lounge

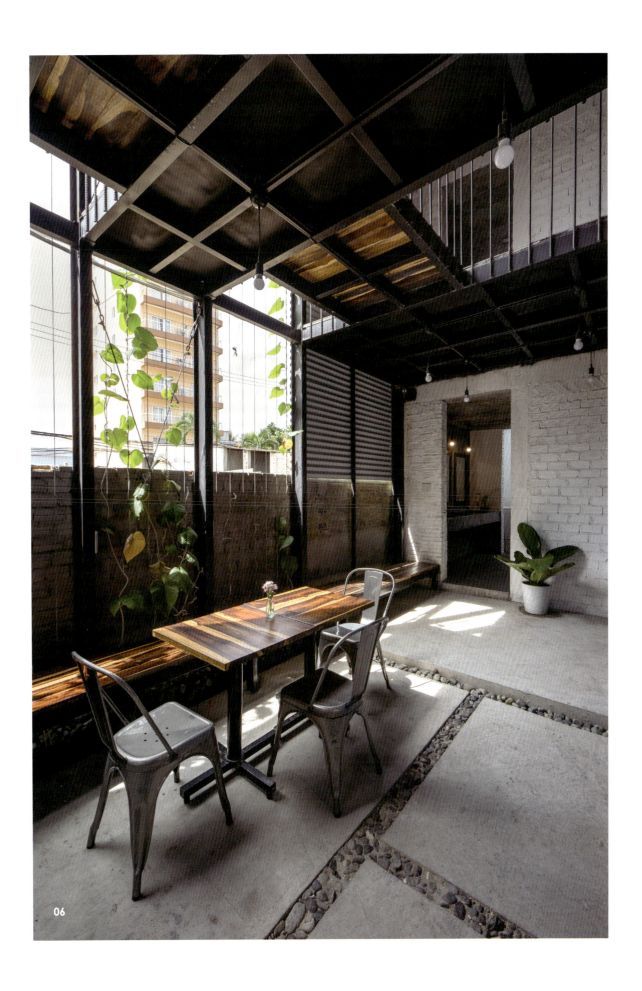

06

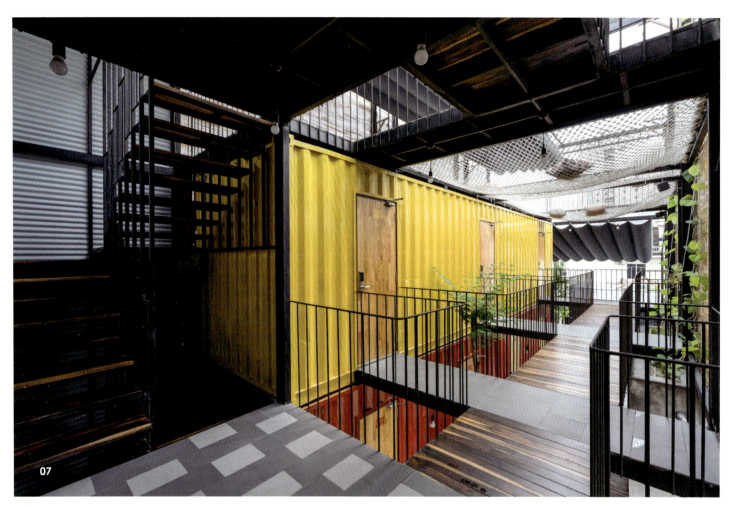

07 / Exterior of lodging
08 / Interior of lodging
09 / Toilet and shower
10 / Top floor

10

Vehicle Charging Station

Location Dongguan, China **Area** 3391 square feet (315 square meters) **Completion date** 2016
Design STAXBOND Buildings Technology Company Limited. **Photography** Apollo **Client** Doedo

01

With the low-carbon economy becoming an important theme in China's economic development, electric vehicles have gradually become a new energy strategy and a crucial part of a well-designed grid. The modular building of the container and the prefabricated building model are closely linked to the low-carbon environmental theme. The project's design aimed to create a fun yet chic area for charging electric vehicles as well as provide facilities for other services, such as rest and motor maintenance.

The building takes dark gray and lemon yellow as its main colors, creating a strong visual impact. Yellow, being a bright color often used for traffic signs, helps draw attention to the building. The dark gray gives the building a sleek high-end look, yet the hints of yellow keep the grayish exterior from appearing too cold and drab.

The building is separated into two floors. At the foot of the structure, long bright lines draw motorists' attention and provide convenient parking spaces. The roof styled like a sports car and sleek windows on the sides naturally evoke a feeling of speed and power. The skylight on top of the building gives off plenty of light for the interior two-story lounge. Contrasted with grey roof, the longue is simple yet stylish.

01 / Front perspective
02 / Back perspective

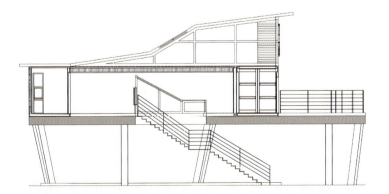
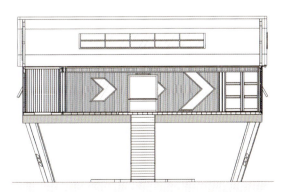

Elevations

03 / Automobile charging area
04-05 / Second floor waiting room

Alphaville Store

Location Araçatuba, Brazil **Area** 1313 square feet (122 square meters) **Completion date** 2014
Design contain[it]+SuperLimão Studio **Photography** MaíraAcayaba

01

Contain[it] and SuperLimão Studio worked together to design Alphaville, a real estate sales office meant to raise the bar for temporary structures. The current architectural trend in Brazil is to either build high-end buildings attractive to the public or simple structures that can be easily reused as needed. The designers wanted to accomplish both.

Alphaville sells real estate lots in phases, which in practice means frequently a sales office is demolished shortly after it is built then rebuilt in a nearby area. Needless to say, the process is exceptionally costly and generates no small amount of environmental waste. Furthermore, Alphaville faces the logistical headaches of coordinating construction and reconstruction of offices throughout the country. To address these challenges, a reusable structure was produced in contain[it]'s factory that could be moved and reassembled throughout Alphaville's properties with minimal effort.

Cross-sectional drawing

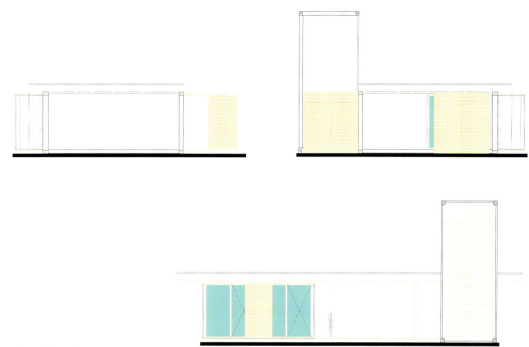

Cross-sectional drawing

01 / Front perspective
02 / Back perspective

The project is made up of three modules, which provide all the functions needed for a sales team: a customer service area, an office/kitchen, and restrooms. If needed, each of these modules can be used separately or recombined to create new structural spaces. Reusability was an important factor that was considered during the design process. Shipping containers had both a structural and logistical function in the project, seeing that all components for the project were shipped on site in these containers.

The choice of materials, such as wood, played off the natural landscape, helping to make the building appear part of the area, rather than merely a transient structure. Positioning the containers vertically allows the sales office to be easily seen in the distance and provides room for a water tank. Since the construction was entirely dry, making the process efficient and relatively waste-free.

The result of this project is a new approach towards temporary sales offices in Brazil that breaks existing paradigms. The key successes of the project include the reuse of raw materials, the centralized production process at contain[it]'s factory, and the simple low-intervention assembly.

03

03-04 / Details
05 / Alphaville store

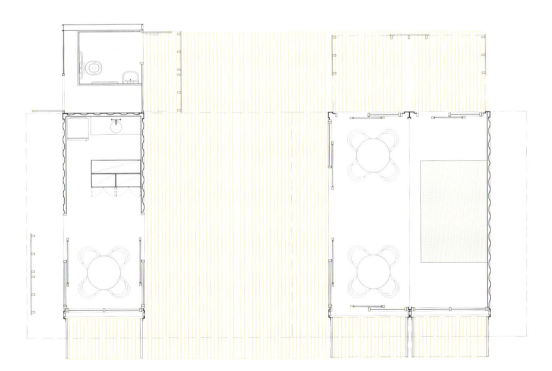

Plan

05

Estoril Praia Clube

Location Estoril, Portugal **Area** 3229 square feet (300 square meters) **Completion date** 2009
Design Ilona Galant, Yaroslav Galant **Photography** Dima Kornilov

Yaroslav Galant made use of an eclectic structure made of five shipping containers to design a building for the Portuguese Football Club (Grupo Desportivo Estoril Praia). Clube 39, as the building is called, is a dynamic structure built on top of an existing building. The project space is made up of offices and connects to adjoining facilities, such as a restaurant, training center, conference hall, and museum.

Founded in 1939, the "Estoril Praia" club has a long story of traditions and achievements. The symbolic name and interiors of Clube 39 instill emotions and esthetics of the mid-century 20th century, such as a bar in a 3D Mondrian style and walls with visuals and Bauhaus panels in office. The eclectic yet familiar visual elements create a comfortable friendly atmosphere, uniting different generations under a logo of the club.

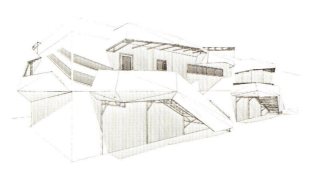

Cross-sectional drawing

The key design goals in the project were simplicity, strong wind resistance, energy efficiency, and environmental sustainability. To accomplish these goals, the design team chose a parametrical roof, which reduced the head wind by 95%. The remaining 5% was funneled into the building, providing natural ventilation, eliminating the need for air conditioning. Moreover, the wooden parametrical roofing creates shade all around the building. Given the unique shape of the roof, these shadows morph and travel around the building over the course of the day.

01 / Front perspective
02 / Detail
03 / Side perspective
04 / Estoril Praia Clube

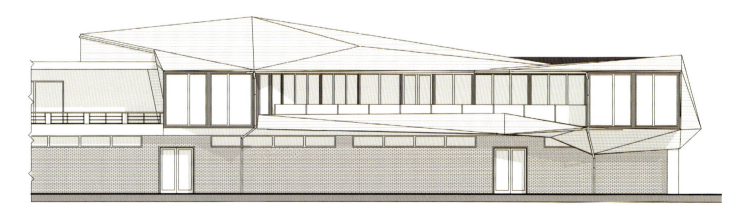

sectional axonometric drawing

05

06

05 / Dining room
06 / Bathroom
07 / Meeting area
08 / Rest area

CRE-Box

Location Shanghai, China **Area** 29,063 square feet (2,700 square meters) **Completion date** 2016
Design Shanghai Kefan Investment Co.,Ltd. **Photography** Wang Xiyong

01

CRE-Box is built to act as a social hub in Shanghai with the goal of attracting entrepreneurs, innovators, and creative events. The project is located at what was formerly the Songhu Railway Jiangwan Station near Wenshui East Road and Guangji Road. It was the first large-scale railway station in China that was formally put into operation. At that time, maritime materials were transported to the urban area via Songhu Railway, and consequently, the railway made an important contribution to the economic and social development of Shanghai. After a four-month renovation, the old station is now turned into a brand-new fashionable multi-functional container plaza.

Twelve containers and two carriages are used for CRE-Box. In the original design, the containers under the bridge were double-decked, but due to the inevitable vibrations that would be created when subway cars passed along the railroad tracks there had to be a minimum 6.5-foot (2-meter) clearance underneath the bridge. As a result, the containers under the bridge were all individually designed in order to replace the previous structural design during the final renovations.

Instead of demolishing the building in the corner of the site, which has now become its own hub called The Beehive, a container plate wraps around the exterior wall of the original concrete building. In this fashion, the building and the entire container plaza present a unified appearance. This not only greatly reduced the cost of transformation, but also added some color and a touch of fashion to the surrounding environment.

Design sketches

01 / Side view
02 / Containers under bridge

02

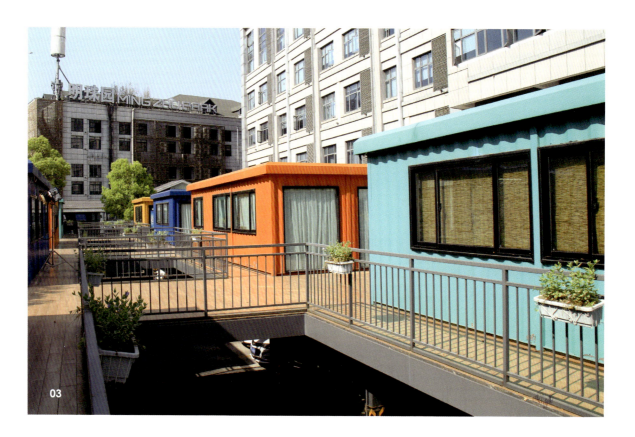

03-05 / Exteriors of container shops

Wisdom Bay

Location Shanghai, China **Area** 53820 square feet (5000 square meters) **Completion date** 2016
Design Shanghai Kefan Investment Co.,Ltd. **Photography** Wang Xiyong

01

Wisdom Bay is a typical example of reducing the damage to the existing base, making efficient use of urban gray space, and making rational use of used freight containers.

The project site was originally a Baoshan industrial base and has been gradually transformed into a part of the growing city. Built on what was originally a parking lot, the first floor was built on stilts to retain the parking and vegetation. In order to meet the different needs of the companies, the designers strived to make the layout flexible so that all regions are relatively independent yet somehow connected with each other. In addition, large-scale outdoor platforms were added to enhance the interaction. The area below the elevated platforms was an underutilized urban space. When describing this area, people would likely to use words such as 'gloomy' and 'dirty.' The designers tried to break this stereotype by using a moveable modular container to add a new spatial configuration to the park, enhancing the value of the space. The design not only preserved the site's original function, but also expanded the office space and improved the land utilization. This is a new exploring ways of changing the nature and functions of passive urban space.

The central design focus for this project is mobility. The project introduces temporary buildings into these sparse parking spaces and creates gardens in the park. By using recycled containers as prefabricated buildings to build two-story and three-story buildings, the designers hoped to address the common issue with traditional construction techniques of inappropriate and inefficient waste disposal. Most of the space inside the container units is used for offices, but space is also reserved for other purposes, such as meeting rooms, studios, and exhibition halls. During the design of the container working space, the designers paid attention to the functional design of each corner, construct complementary functions

02

among each area, fully integrating with people's work habits. All of the areas — work halls, recreation areas, fitness trails, football stadiums and the specialized brainstorming meeting rooms — are well laid out to enhance the alertness of the employees and to ensure the office environment is neither dull nor depressing. The container space integrates the functions of the conference room, the reception hall and the rooftop lounge all into one place. With three large glass windows, the space conveys a sense of togetherness and rejects seclusion. In addition, the large French windows ensure that sunshine can reach the deepest parts of the building during the day, minimizing the need for lights. Being environmentally friendly and highly mobile are the two best features of the container office.

A high-performance thermal insulation panel sandwiched in the walls of the container and container frame helps the building withstand climate as harsh as Scandinavia's. These sandwich panels are fastened directly to the container frame, such as windows, roofing elements and floors.

Plumping, electricity and air-conditioning have been installed from the outside, made to be easily disassembled as needed.

03

04

The container's color-coded design is the most striking aspect of the office area. Each container area was painted in one of four vibrant colors, from dark green to light yellow. The colorful restaurant contrasts with the gray surroundings and environment. The colors match those seen on container ships, helping to stimulate people's creativity.

In addition, the designers made shrewd use of the space around the original building, extending the area of the original building with containers. The extended sections serve as dining, leisure, entertainment, and other commercial venues. The rapid construction of container buildings not only saves on cost, but also reduces the impact of construction on the surrounding environment.

01 / Side view
02 / Panorama
03 / Design sketch
04 / View from street
05 / Side view
06 / Deck
07 / Walkway
08-10 / Interior

11-12 / Interior view
13 / Shop

Pop Brixton

Location Brixton, South London **Area** 21,528 square feet (2000 square meters) **Completion date** 2015
Design Carl Turner Architects **Photography** Tim Crocker **Client** Lambeth Council

A new micro-city of community and culture, Pop Brixton in South London has revitalized what was once an abandoned space of around 21528 square feet (2000 square meters) into a bustling hub of activity, offering much needed work to the area as well as an affordable leisure spot for locals. The venue boasts restaurants, bars, café, exhibition spaces, studios, workshops, as well as an open public space to meet and socialize.

The goal of the project was to create a flexible space that could evolve with the community around it. As such, the design team chose to use shipping containers, given they are inexpensive and lightweight, allowing simple changes to the layout in the future as needed.

The layout provides a mix of 20-foot (6-meter) and 40-foot (12-meter) containers, each tailored to bespoke specifications, depending on the tenants' requirements. All of the units are fully insulated and come equipped with power outlets, overhead lighting, double glazed windows, and high-speed internet access.

The landscaping strategy was an integral part of the project, which links the site to the street and wider public region around Brixton Station Road. This area includes a community garden with a greenhouse, an orchard, and herb beds where members of the public can learn about urban farming. At the center of the site, a tremendous polytunnel, raised on top of the containers, provides seating for diners.

The commission was won through an open competition process to design, deliver and run the project for three years minimum. The design firm has acted as the architect, developer, curator and creator for the whole project, having spearheaded the vision from the start, including raising funds. The resultant architecture is a truly collaborative and

01/Front perspective

inclusive space that perfectly demonstrates CTA's approach to creating places: design spaces that respond to the local context and allow individuality and creativity to thrive. The project was in partnership with the Lambeth Council, conceived as an incubator for local talent with over 70% of tenants from the area.

Pop Brixton now has over 50 independent businesses operating at the site, with around 200 people working there every day, and has attracted between 10,000 and 15,000 people per week during the summer months.

Stereogram

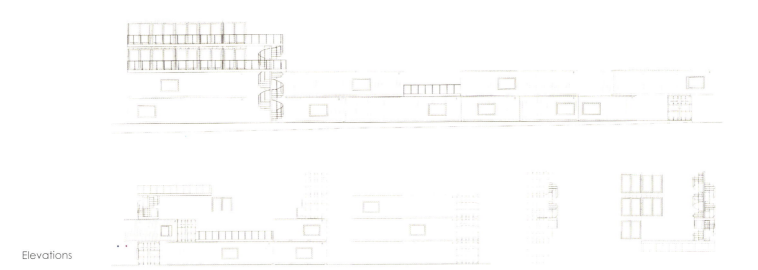

Elevations

02

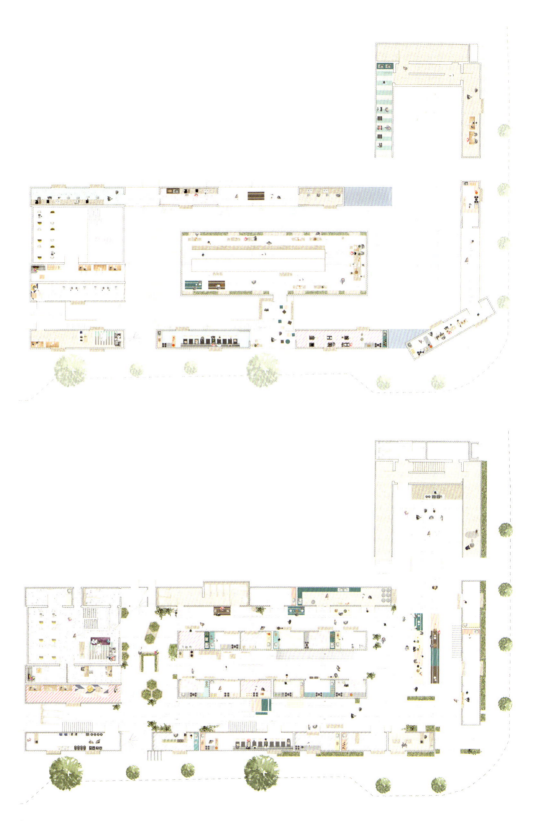

Plans

02 / Staircase

Unit Cafe

Location Kiev, Ukraine **Area** 2960 square feet (275 square meters) **Completion date** 2016
Design TSEH Architectural Group **Photography** Mihail Cherny, Evgen Zuzovsky
Client Vasyl Khmelnytsky's fund – K.Fund

01

The café was designed as a part of a larger revitalization project in Kiev, built for students who study at an IT school called the "Unit Factory." Originally, the team considered building a café within the school, but as the project went on, it became clear there would not be enough space. Consequently, the designers decided to locate a café outside of the main building.

The whole project was incredibly simple. Just 14 freight containers were used in the implementation of the project. One of the major advantages of using containers is speed. The whole construction only took two and half months. Another strength of containers is that they are significantly cheaper than building with standard materials. However, the most important thing containers brought to the project is their energy. Containers are unusual, bright and striking.

Inside, the ground and first floor have comfortable sofas, tables with chairs and plants. There is a kitchen, a lavatory and pantries on the first floor. The total area of the cafe is 2960 square feet (275 square meters).

Given the client's high standards for environmental sustainability, several strategies were employed to reduce the energy consumption of the building. The entire structure is well insulated, even though the container itself appears untouched. In addition to insulation, all of the containers have been specially prepared, coated with anti-corrosive compounds and modified to be waterproof

The team managed to use shipping containers in a new way and build a magnificent caté in the process The café has become a hot spot. Students as well as locals all frequent the café to eat, have meetings, discuss business, and to chat. in the territory of Unit City-- the name that was given to the territory of the revitalization.

01 / Front perspective
02 / Entrance

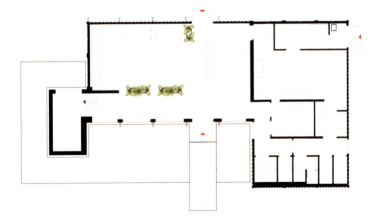

First-floor plan

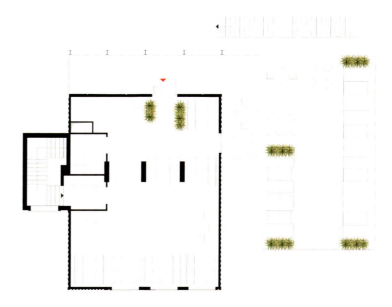

Plan

05

THE KRANE

Location Copenhagen. Denmark **Area** 3078 square feet (286 square meters) **Completion date** 2017
Design Arcgency **Photography** Rasmus Hjortshøj - COAST Studio **Client** Klaus Kastbjerg

01

The project is more a hybrid. The two containers on ground are ISO hc, 40 feet. The containers on ground contains the foyer, catering kitchen, space for bikes and an outdoor shower.

For the functions we needed space and something that would not disturb the compositions of the crane. The container was an obvious choice because of it's heritage as an industrial object you see in every harbour.

THE KRANE re-defines luxury in a hideaway for two where the art is the view

THE KRANE is an immersive, multi-sensory experience. Inside is exclusive Danish design in black in homage to its past as a coal crane. Outside is the sea, sky, harbour and panoramic views over Copenhagen. An inventive, cohesive concept in this private retreat for two.

There's a story behind how the crane became THE KRANE. Kastbjerg, a passionate, pivotal figure driving numerous projects on Copenhagen's waterfronts, such as Paper Island (PapirØen), THE SILO, HARBOUR HOUSE and THE SIGNING ROOM, explains it best. "The harbour came with two cranes. When Paustian first opened its doors, they were having a big reception and the architect Jørn Utzon, who also designed the Sydney Opera House, asked if we could please move the crane to a more beautiful position. As Jørn stood on the quay directing us, we lifted the crane right there and then and moved it to the perfect spot. ."

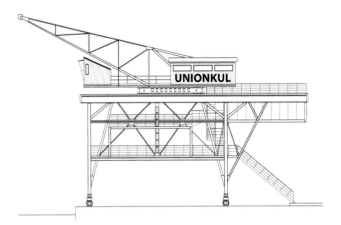

Elevation

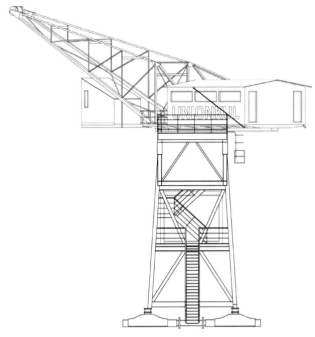

01 / Front perspective
02 / Panorama

Step inside THE KRANE and you'll instantly sense a re-definition of luxury deep in the Danish DNA. An understated elegance with only the essentials. It's all part of the vision, where the focus has been the integration of sensations - sight, sound and stemning (the Danish word for atmosphere). So we optimised the inside to capture natural daylight and set the stage for the views of the water outside. Curating the perfect materials and carefully calibrating how the light reflects the surfaces and how that impacts the way people perceive their surroundings. Then there's the water outside. In Denmark, during the summer we have longer days of sunlight from about 5 am till 10 pm. Along the coastline, the light is very soft and diffused. From inside THE KRANE, even stormy weather looks amazing."

In addition to its allusions to coal, black plays a pivotal role in muting and minimising visual distractions so people feel almost enveloped in the interior. At the same time, black dramatizes the changing light and breath-taking views outside. For Møller, black isn't just black. "There are hundreds of different shades of black. Depending on the time of day, you can see so many subtle nuances."

In terms of location, THE KRANE is exclusive yet inclusive. Whether you're renting the living space, spa, meeting room or reception area, you're removed from the city without feeling too remote, yet close to the pulse of the city just minutes away. "It's rare to find a harbour like this in Denmark," explains Kastbjerg, "Nordhavn still has an industrial look and feel that's attracting entrepreneurs, artisans and others. We kept that rough, industrial feeling and added something unexpected. An old engine room that's now a high-end retreat where you can enjoy champagne and a spectacular view. Now that's luxury."

While other cities renovate areas overlooked and end up eliminating appealing aspects of their past, THE KRANE honours its past with a new reason for being. "How can you tell your kids about an old industrial port if there's nothing left of it? New buildings don't have the same charm or story to tell."

Enjoy this unconventional angle on luxury that's upscale yet down to earth. Raw yet refined. With enviable views of light and the water outside as the centrepiece inside. A refreshing take on escape in the form of a private getaway - where you're the only guests

03

03-05 / Details

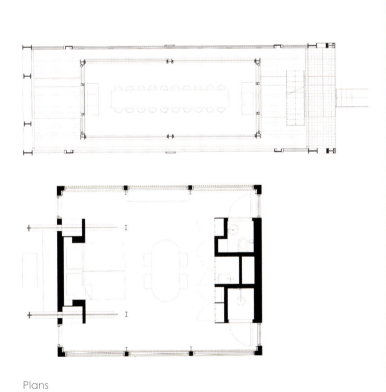

Plans

05

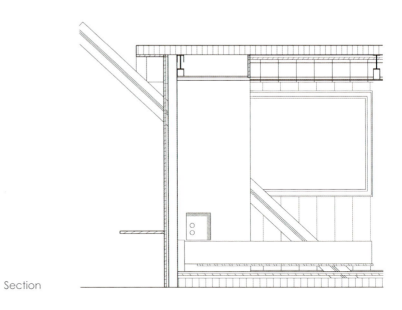

Section

06 / Detail
07-09 / Bathroom

Nike Unlimited Rio

Location Rio de Janeiro, Brazil **Area** 6458 square feet (600 square meters) **Completion date** 2016
Design GTM Cenografia **Photography** Eduardo Biermann, Renato Frasnelli **Client** Nike. Inc.

01

The concept and creative direction came from Nike, focusing on their campaign for the 2016 Rio Olympics. They started the process by presenting their ideas, goals and references. GTM collaborated with creative and technical expertise, creating concept sketches and producing the fabrication and final assembly. Together, Nike and GTM put their ideas first on paper, then in tests and pre-assembly, and finally in construction.

Nike's primary request was to offer a content experience that would serve as a catalyst for the consumer to engage with Nike's products and services. Another desire was to have a large LED screen to draw attention and communicate some messages.

An initial goal was to communicate the categories (soccer, sportswear, basketball, etc) trategic points through trials and digital experiences.

Inspired by containers and minimalism, the project was divided into two areas to offer a journey to consumers. In order to accommodate the exhibition for high circulation, large sheds modeled after freight containers were constructed. The shed were outfitted with a metal structure and double trapezoidal metallic tiles with heat treatment.

The lateral extremities received translucent polycarbonate plates to enhance natural lighting and the sides were accented with a diagonal cut with embedded LED lighting.

Given the industrial inspiration and technological features in the design, the interior space was predominantly white with cement and wooden floors. The black lining is a neutral color, which helps to emphasize the individual internal elements.

A colorful tunnel with LED panels on the floor stands out at the entrance of the first section, displaying different types of products, such as global football boots and running shoes. Consumers had also the opportunity to take pictures to be share on social networks wearing the iconic NikeLab Team Brazil Medal Stand Jacket, in which Brazilian athletes received their Olympic medals on podium.

In the other section, the furniture has a mostly white metallic structure with built-in led lighting, highlighting the products that were on sale. To complete the retail experience, the designers included on site a big cashier counter and an area to customize t-shirts.

On the outside, also in white, LED lights color the facade perimeter with a gradient of colors, creating dynamic cube visual effects.

The central LED cube, an installation of Brazilian artist and designer Muti Randolph, provided a colorful graphic projection that celebrated epic moments during the competition.

The iron and aluminum structure was 39 feet (12 meters) high, 33 feet (10 meters) long and 33 feet(10 meters) wide, made up of was 840 LED plates fixed in 84 columns controlled by 14 motors. The project, built in a highly public venue, was a unique to celebrate one of the world's most important and well-known events.

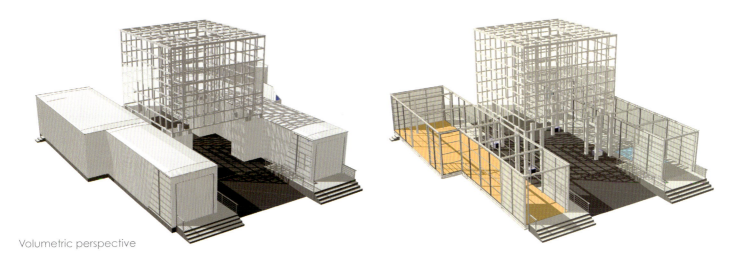

Volumetric perspective

01 / Side view
02 / Container entrance

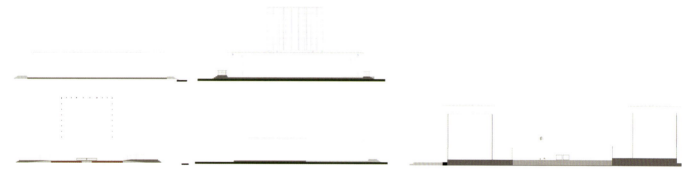

Elevations

03 / Container exit
04 / Side view
05 / RIO letters next to container building

MaxHaus Paulista

Location Sao Paulo, Brazil **Area** 3879 square feet (360 square meters) **Completion date** 2013
Design GTM Cenografia **Photography** GTM CENOGRAFIA

In 2013, the exhibition planner and design firm GTM Cenografia was commissioned to design a sales office for MaxHaus. The client is a Brazilian company dealing in residential buildings, specializing in apartments with a complete open plan, to offer flexibility for the owner to rearrange the living space as desired. The concept became the staring point in GTM's design process. The end product was a design that was bold, adaptable and fast to build: a painted container building with finishes ready to use such, as cement boards, vinyl flooring, wooden deck, and carpeting.

The designers wanted a concept with an urban feel. For this goal, they brought in artist Loro Verz who decorated the interior and exterior with graffiti art.. In an online interview, Loro said the client gave him all the freedom to create and paint whatever he thought would work best, which links back to the flexibility embodied within MaxHaus' brand.

Being forward-thinking and having extensive construction expertise, GTM decided to pre-fabricate a model to test what problems might arise during installation on site. Consequently, when the containers reached their final destination, the construction was much faster, cleaner and accurate, especially since containers were the main structural element.

The office building has three floors. The ground floor contains two balconies, a welcome area, a projection room, a customer service area, a media room, a kitchen, and restrooms. The second floor contains a conference room, a room for realtors, and a lounge. Finally, the third floor contains a storage room and another room for realtors.

In managing circulation, visitors navigated to the different section through the stairs. In addition, on the third floor, a footbridge connects both sides of the building, allowing visitors to view the whole site

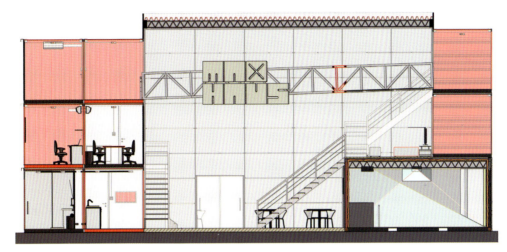

Cross-section 1

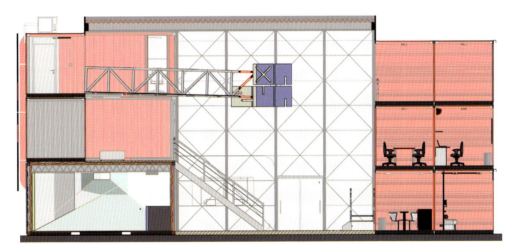

Cross-section 2

02

01 / Sales stand
02 / Facade illustration

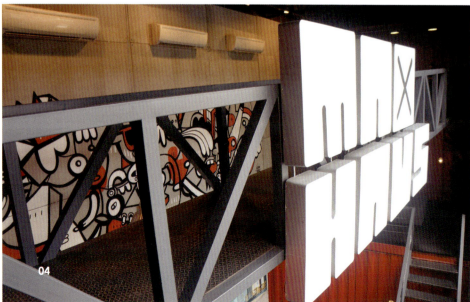

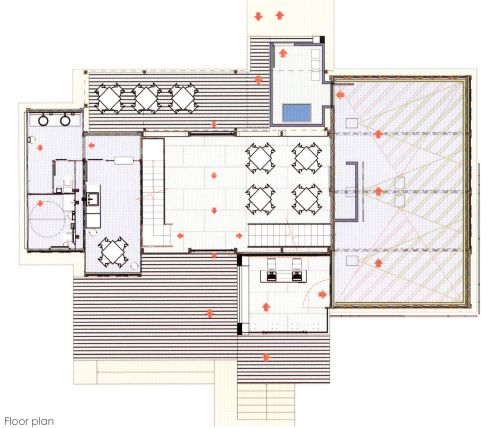

Floor plan

03 / Central atrium with Loro Verz graffiti art
04 / Footbridge
05 / Internal lounge illustration

HATAGOYA EBISU HOTEL

Location Osaka, Japan **Area** 753 square feet (70 square meters) **Completion date** 2017
Design Atelier Mugi Architect Office/IDMobile co.,LTD **Photography** Kei Sugino **Client** Ryu Arin

In recent years, the number of foreign tourists in Osaka has been rapidly increasing. In order to meet the rising demand for accommodations, the client wanted a hotel specifically targeting overseas travelers. The site was a downtown area where simple accommodations for day laborers were concentrated and many of such lodgings had already been converted into facilities for foreign tourists. However, not a small number of them were operating illegally. The client wanted legitimate accommodations, allowing for sustainable long-term operations, and safeguards against earthquakes, given these are a common occurrence in Japan.

Although the region is not particularly clean, the area is still tinged with an old Showa-era atmosphere, something that has all but disappeared in contemporary Japan, making Osaka an attraction for tourists. Given the site's context, we adopted containers for the following reasons: provides a design with a distinctive personality, low cost, and able to safely endure seismic activity.

The two-storied building consists of 12 shipping containers, each 20 feet (6 meters) in length. A group of eight containers cover the front of the site, another group of four in the back, and the space between the two forms the common area. The common area melds seamlessly with the external area, making the space feel very open. In particular, on the west side of the common area on the first floor is an open space with double-height structure, which is designed to be a shared living space for guests. Smoothly connecting the common area with the other areas of the building is a set of roji, a traditional path in Japanese gardens that leads to a tea ceremony. Due to its small size, the roji allows a little privacy within the public space. Conversely, strict privacy is given to the offices and guest rooms and, as such, the spaces are detached from the overall common area There are two types of rooms: one for families using two container units and the other with a single or double bed made up of just one container unit. The building has a total of seven rooms.

01 / Nighttime view from south side

Originally, the team was requested to add a residence space for the client, but it ultimately was not possible due to budget constraints. Therefore, the team only built the part of the hotel part that could be operated as accommodation and planned later on, when the client has earned enough revenue from the hotel, to add a third floor for the client to live on.

Most of the Japanese design seen throughout the site, such as shoji and garden stones, were created and installed by the owner, who took advantage of the handmade look container units can provide.

The team looked into purchasing a neighboring site and extending the building in the future. If followed through, containers would work quite well in constructing an expansion. The project is a building as the first step for such prospective plan.

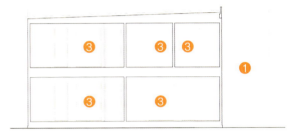

Cross-section

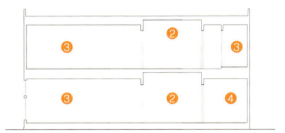

1 Approach
2 Common area
3 Guest room
4 Office

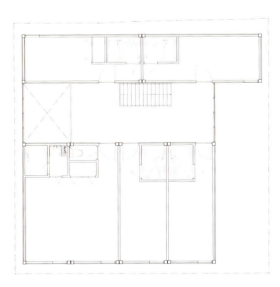

First-floor plan

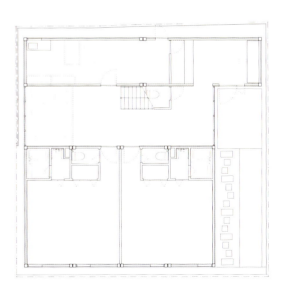

Second-floor plan

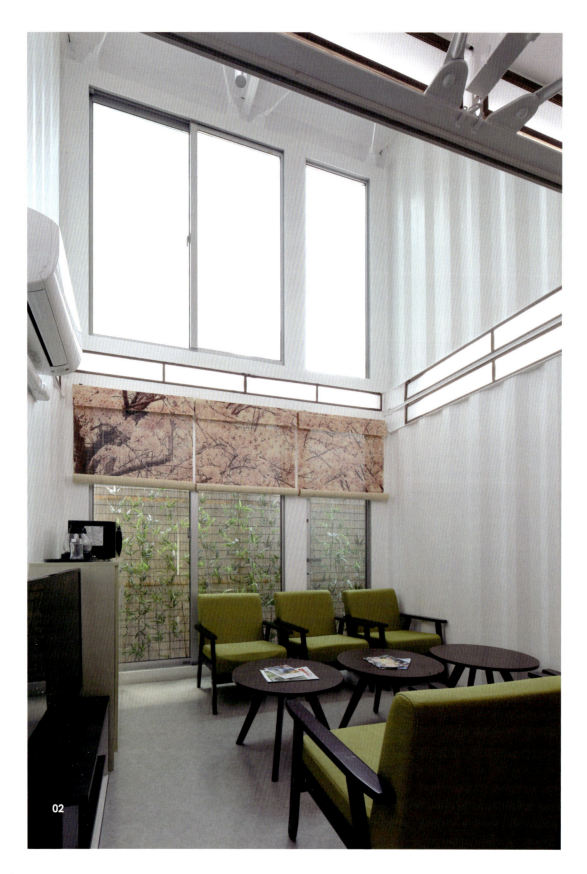

02 / Double-height common area
03 / First-floor common area
04 / Second-floor common area
05 / Guest room

Bonaire Street Market

Location Bonaire (Valencia) **Completion date** 2017 **Design** MESURA Partners in Architecture & vdv / **Photography** Salva López

Located in the outskirts of Valencia, the Bonaire Street Market is a makeshift group of food stalls in the middle of a parking lot for a shopping mall. The Bonaire Street Market embraces a dining trend becoming ever more popular: street food.

The client had wanted an outdoor eating area. The space given to work with — a parking lot — was by no means a comfortable place to have lunch. Thus, the team decided to build a 'foodie oasis' in the parking lot, partitioned off by walls made of freight containers and pallets. The result is an isolated and peaceful space in contrast with the nearby shopping mall.

A key goal in the project was to cultivate a Mediterranean atmosphere. To do this, the designers decorated the space with plants, pergolas and small tables. In addition, several local artists painted the containers with dynamic images, giving them a look both distinctive yet still very much Mediterranean. Restaurant chains, such as Sorsi and Moorsi, Curry Corner, and La Llorona Onion, have all set up stalls in the Bonaire Street Market, making the space a fantastic culinary experience.

01 / Front side perspective
02 / Elevated view

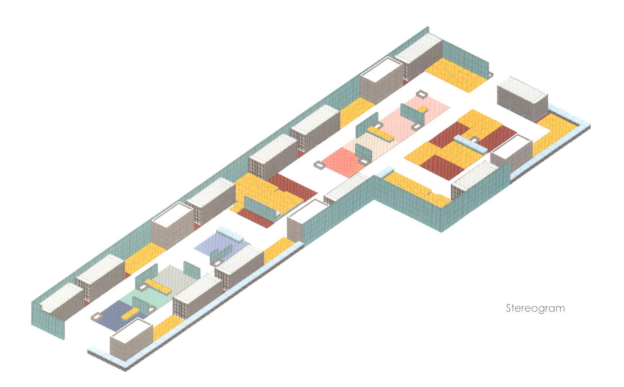

Stereogram

Plan

Zhengda Colorful City Container Residence Design

Location Gu Village, Shanghai, China **Area** 775 square feet (72 square meters) **Completion date** 2017
Design Shanghai HuaDu Architecture and Urban Design Group (HDD) Haiao Zhang
Photography Shengliang SU

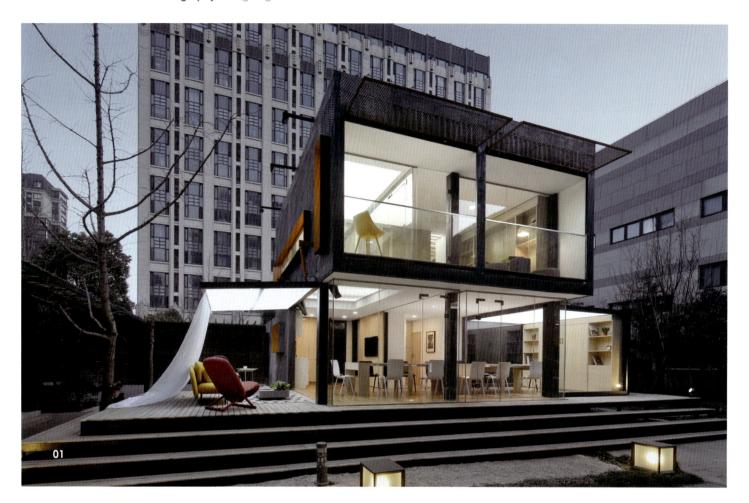

01

The client was a young entrepreneur starting up a 3D printing business in Shanghai who wanted a place to work and live that was relatively inexpensive. The client rented out for four shipping containers and had us transform them into his office and home.

DESIGN STRATEGY: Transform Space Based on Need

Given the malleable nature of shipping containers, we could arrange containers in different ways. In the future, one might even build container buildings the same way one plays LEGO. This is a new way of living and working. Based on the situation, the space can adapt accordingly. The project consists of three modes to shift between: life mode, work mode, and relax mode.

Life Mode

In the living mode, the house has double-height living room. A bed can be folded down. A well-equipped kitchen and restroom are available as well. All day-to-day needs can be fulfilled in this mode. The client can live with his family during this mode.

Work Mode

As a startup company, the team needed multiple different kinds of space to work in. In the work mode, the whole layout of the building changes to accommodate a work environment. A hidden table can be pulled out as a reception table. The foldable floor can add on whole extra meeting room for the upper level. By folding the bed on the upper floor, one can get a whole new office room. The restroom can transform into a place for brainstorming. By folding out one of the wall, one can get an outside gathering area. The table can be stretched from 6.6 feet (2 meters) to 26 feet (8 meters), useful when conducting large meetings..

01 / Street frontage
02 / Side view

Relaxation Mode

One can switch to the relaxation mode by opening a wall and pulling out a shipping container. With this arrangement, one can have an extremely long space well-suit for all sorts of recreational activities, such BBQs and dinner parties.

HDD also took care to protect all plants on site so that the building and nature could live harmoniously together. In the back yard, a simple triangular installation is designed for meditation. It is 19.6 feet (6 meters) off the ground in order to avoid blocking sunlight. Combined with the metallic and reflective appearance, one can get meditative experience inside.

With industrial pre-production, components can be pre-made in a factory then sent to the site. In the future, even more possibilities might be available. Renovation of container boxes is just the tip of iceberg for huge renovation projects over the next ten years in China. HDD is trying to solve the Chinese housing shortage by using pre-fab technology.

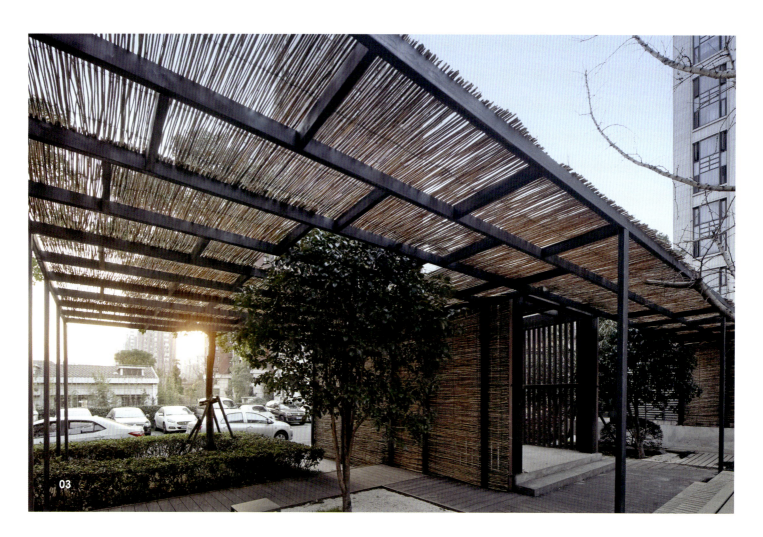

03 / Canopy
04 / Side view
05 / View of dining area from outside

Axonometric view

Sectional view

06 / Folding panel
07-08 / Interior view

Plan

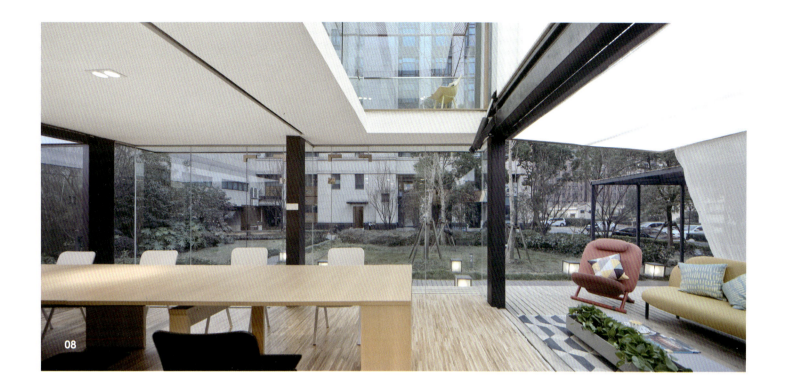

Possible configurations first floor

09 / Interior view
10 / Side view

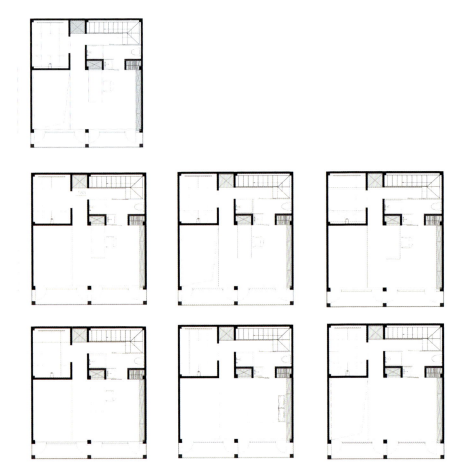

Possible configurations of second floor

Plugin Tower

Location Shenzhen, China **Area** 1076 square feet (100 square meters) **Completion date** 2016
Design People's Architecture Office (He Zhe, James Shen, Zang Feng)
Photography People's Architecture Office,Hannah Wu
Client China Vanke Co., LTD. &LDG Narrative Design

01

Every year, Vanke, a major real estate developer in China, holds an event soliciting architects to submit designs addressing an important contemporary architectural issue. In 2016, Vanke invited People's Architecture Office to tackle the 'future of housing' through an experimental built work. Installed at Vanke's headquarters in Shenzhen, the Plugin Tower addresses the insecurity of private home ownership in a country where the government exclusively controls land and the construction of private homes is reserved for the very wealthy.

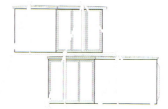

North Elevation   East Elevation

01-02 / Exterior
03-04 / Details

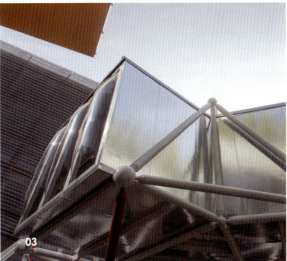

05

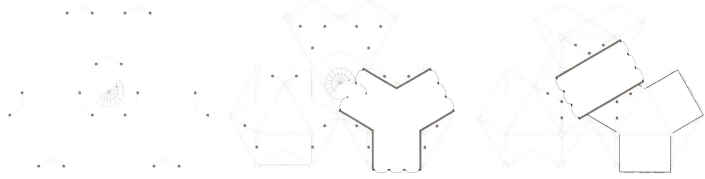

First-floor plan   Second-floor plan   Third-floor plan

The Plugin Tower reduces the costs and logistical planning necessary for building a home because there is no risk of losing one's property: if forced to relocate, residents can pack up their homes and bring it with them. Classified as a temporary structure, the Plugin Tower does not require an underground foundation, thereby circumventing the strict planning approval for permanent structures, further simplifying the building process

A multistory prefab system is infinitely expandable. Inspired by Metabolism, the Plugin Tower consists of a steel space frame and a kit of parts that can be reassembled in endless variations. Empty bays within the frame are plugged with living units that can be altered and unplugged when necessary. Units are made with a proprietary Plugin Panel system created by People's Architecture Office, made up of modules incorporate insulation, wiring, plumbing, as well as interior and exterior finishes into one molded part. Panels attached with integrated locks can be easily installed by a couple of unskilled workers with just a hex wrench. Living spaces can be added without heavy machinery and the layouts of the building are not restricted to the shape of a box.

In contrast to the instability of housing in China, the 'future of housing' proposed by People's Architecture Office is a flexible design that adapts to changing needs and fluctuating conditions.

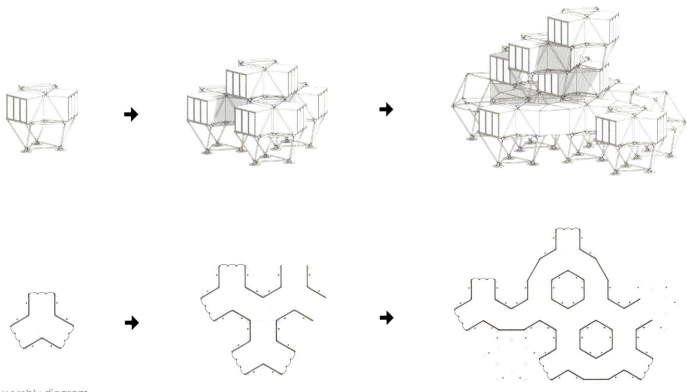

Assembly diagram

05 / Interior
06 / Hypothetical usage of building

Módulos habitacionales temporales

Location Nogales, Chile **Area** 3767 square feet (350 square meters) **Completion date** 2015
Design Felipe Ehrenfeld L.,Ignacio Orfali H., Ignacio Prieto I. **Photography** Felipe Ehrenfeld L.

01

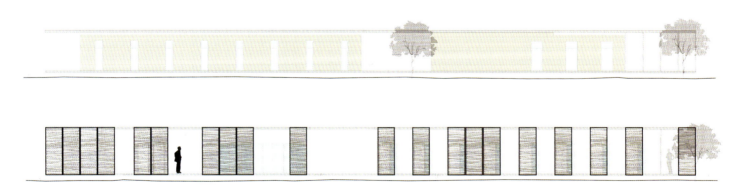

Cross-sectional

Located in the town of Nogales in the Valparaíso region of Chile, a rural area where agricultural activities predominate and farming is part of the landscape, this area has a Mediterranean climate typical of central Chile, characterized by a prolonged dry season between the months of September and April.

An agricultural company gave the design team the task of building accommodations to house 32 temporary workers (temporeros) from the months October to March. The accommodations had to include a kitchen, a dining hall, bathrooms, bedroom, and living areas. The space had to be relatively simple and easy to maintain. The building had to be placed in a predefined location, adjacent to where agricultural activities were routinely carried out, fully exposed to sunlight. To design the project, the team had 10 shipping containers of 20 feet (6 meters).

In developing this project, the local climate was an essential factor to consider, given that temperatures routinely reach 35 ° C during the day. For this reason, it was important that the end of the working day, the workers could return to a shady and cool enclosure with basic conditions for good habitability throughout the seasons.

On top of all this, the whole operation had to be efficient since the budget was limited to only $450 USD per square meter. Given the restrictions placed on the designers, working with the existing shipping containers on-site seemed to be the most sensible and cost-effective option.

01 / Front perspective
02-03 / Details

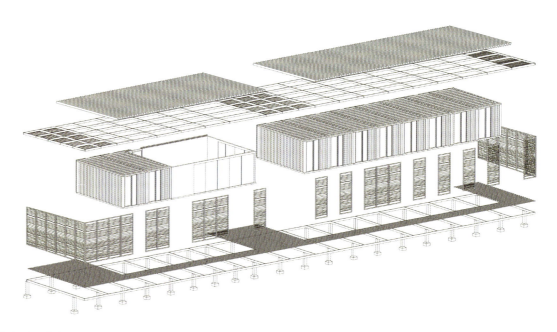

Detached view

03

In planning how to best utilize the shipping containers, the team decided that a rectangular base would both maximize the constructed area and decrease the surface area of the exterior walls. In this sense, the architectural strategy can be defined as establishing a double envelope structure that utilizes its own shadows for shade.

To begin in accomplishing this goal, the main façade was oriented to the south. Towards the north, the façade was drilled with holes, small enough to avoid excessive sunlight yet allows for cross ventilation with the interior enclosures. In addition to this façade, the designers also added layer made of wood placed 1.6 inches (5 centimeters) in between each container, generating further ventilation.

The designers adopted a similar strategy for the roof. A single large with a substantial projection over the eaves cover the whole site. The purpose is to both provide shade as well as dissipate solar heat through vented cover. One exception to the roofing is the courtyards, where Chilean bamboo was used instead in order to create a subtle lighting effect when sunlight filtered through.

This project can be characterized by the centralized arrangement of intimate spaces, such as bathrooms and bedroom, all contained by peripherally located common areas.

03 / Side View
04 / Interior view

05

06

07

05 / Side View
06 / Details
07 / Front perspective

Container Casulo

Location Belo Horizonte Brazil **Area** 301 square feet (28 square meters) **Completion date:** 2015
Design Bernardo Horta Arquiteto, MEIUS Arquitetura, Aerolito Arquitetura **Photography** Jomar Bragança

The Studio Casual is a changeable space, demonstrating how flexible dwellings can be today. The project presents us with different "faces" of the same fixed furniture. What we wanted to create is an interactive and lively place that has a palpable feeling people live here, a space that can be touched and deployed not only at a single glance, but also with one's own curiosity. With simple layouts, new systems are established for different uses, from a salonto to even a small residence. With the advent of new technologies, containers have become more and more common in use.

Alternating mesh pallets, conventionally used handling large quantities of materials, were used as the deck cover. However, the pallets used are much more economical than ordinary wooden pallets, given their ability to be assembled and disassembled as required. Furthermore, the entire material can be reused in case of the site needs to be reconfigured. The choice of shell coating was due to the low cost of this material and the convenience of installation. Bonding thin layers of timber together produces the lip plate. Because of the rapid growth and fast reproduction speed, the material has a high potential for forest management.

Polar fleece used on the walls acts as an environmental-friendly thermal and acoustic insulation. Since it is made from recycled raw material, polar fleece is 100% recyclable. Sustainability is its major advantage because it is produced from recycled PET bottles without any use of resins nor additional water or carbon during the process. Native vegetation was favored in order to create environmentally friendly landscaping. The use of native vegetation stresses the importance of these plants to the climate. Native vegetation has resistance against possible pest attacks and can contribute to the diversity of fauna as food for the local wildlife.

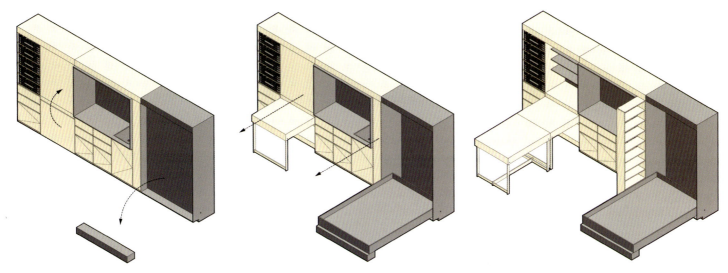

Diagram of pull-out furniture in apartment

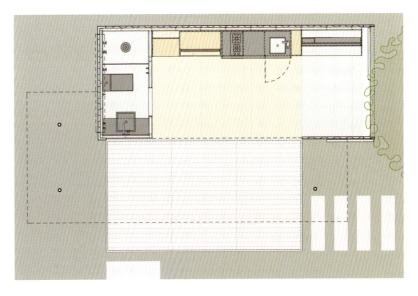

01 / Container Casulo   Floor plan

Contemporary residences require workplaces and adaptable housing. A flexible cabinet offers a wide range of structures and tools that can adapt to the user's choice. All systems shown below can be adapted to a variety of processes and uses. The removable drawers are perfect for keeping files and entire stacks of materials in order. Spacious, easy removal and internal customization make the drawers especially useful for day-to-day use. The removable table can be mounted to multiple locations at user's choice, allowing for simultaneous use with the folding table or used anywhere else. When the table is not in use, it can be fitted to the cabinet body.

Moreover, we also developed an open area where you could place a small desk for a meal. The table layout is simple and can be easily pulled out of the closet. The extra bench enables various kinds of additional uses. A cooktop has been installed in this space to replenish the house. The door cabinet opening below the countertop can house other possibilities, such as a fridge, a wine cellar, or even a closet fitted with casters. A bed built into a closet was developed to easily mesh with the rest of the space. When the bed is closed, the space can be occupied by other activities. The rest of the furniture was removed by our partner, Tok & Stok, for this project.

02 / External view
03 / Bathroom
04 / Deck view

The WFH House

Location Wuxi, China. **Area** 1938 square feet (180 square meters) **Completion date** 2012
Design Arcgency **Photography** Jens Markus Lindhe. Mads Møller. **Client** worldFLEXhome

The concept of the WFH House is a dynamic lodging adapted for local environmental challenges, such as earthquakes, using only 40-foot (12-meter) shipping containers. The overall design is based on Nordic values, namely, flexibility and people-oriented. Everything, from the architecture to the interior embodies these values. As such, the project focuses on providing plenty of natural light, creating components that could be easily disassembled as needed, and using sustainable approaches in construction.

The roof is specially designed for harvesting rainwater, which can be used by the inhabitants for their personal needs. Photovoltaic cells were integrated into the design to be more energy-efficient, allowing the building to produce its own power. Overall, the energy usage of the WFH House is 50% lower than the standard requirements for new housing constructions in Denmark.

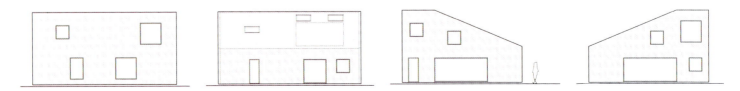

Elevations

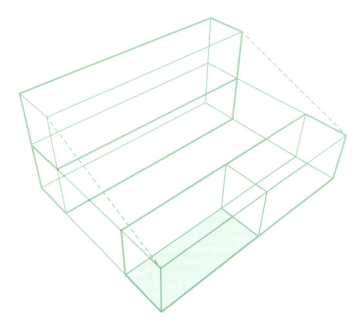

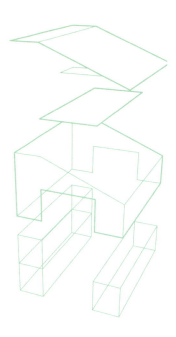

01 / Bamboo facade
02 / Pre-modified container structure

The FLEX space is the heart of the house, containing the living room, kitchen yet can still be used for many other purposes. Parts of the room are double height, bringing plenty of additional lighting. The rest of the FLEX space is one-story high, defined by a landing that leads to the second floor. At the ends of the FLEX space are doors connecting to the surroundings. When the doors are opened, the boundary between inside and outside disappears. This is a fundamental part of the design: to open up and let nature in. Such functionality gives the inhabitant the ability define what actions take place inside as well as outside according their own requirements.

The geometry of the FLEX space is defined by the two rows of containers, which can easily be modified to various sizes. The FLEX space has a number of possible configurations for subdivisions. However, the area can also be one big space, bringing in a lot of light and creating a sense of openness. The kitchen elements are built into the wall, creating more floor space and also making connections to plumbing simpler. The kitchen can also be extended using a freestanding element, defining the work area of the kitchen.

The FLEX space connects to all other spaces in the building, making the area much more compact. It is possible to expand the openings leading from the FLEX space into other rooms, creating flexible solutions within the same system. The landing creates access to the second floor, but can also be used as a recreational space, offering the inhabitant a secluded location, but still enjoy the company of people in the house. It is an ideal place for a quiet retreat and still being able to observe what is going on in the house.

The bedrooms each take up half a container, equally 161 square feet (15 square meters). There are four bedrooms; all can be used for multiple purposes, such as parent's bedroom, children's bedroom, workspace, etc. Three of the rooms have windows on two facades, giving mixed light. The walls facing the FLEX space can be removed, fully or partially, further highlighting the structure's ability to adapt to different needs.

03-04 / WFH House under construction
05 / Interior view

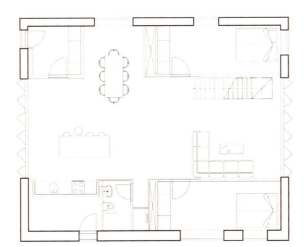
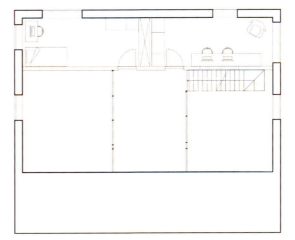

Plans

06

06 / Kitchen
07-08 / Detail

Urban Rigger

Location Copenhagen, Denmark **Area** 45,208 square feet (4,200 square meters) **Completion date** 2014
Design BIG-Bjarke Ingels Group **Photography** Laurent de Carniere, Frederik Lyng
Client Udvikling Danmark A/s

01

In response to the increasing housing demand from student with the Copenhagen area, Urban provides an innovative solution that BIG hopes other ports around the world can learn from. Made from up-cycled shipping containers, Urban Rigger is a floating carbon-neutral property located in Copenhagen's harbor. The project, measuring in total 7319 square feet (680 square meters), consists of 15 living spaces organized around a green courtyard encased in a protective glass shell. Amenities on the property include a kayak landing, a bathing platform, a barbecue area, and a communal roof terrace. Downstairs, below sea level, the pontoon basement features 12 storage areas, a technical room, and a fully automated laundry.

Stacking the containers in a circle allowed the designers to create 12 studio residences with a garden, functioning as a common area for students. Like a houseboat, the student housing is buoyant. The architects state, "In terms of rising sea levels, this is the most resilient form of housing because it moves with the water. It's the only building type that will never flood."

In order to ensure the housing was affordable, a variety of environmentally friendly technologies were incorporated in order to minimize energy usage. Photovoltaic cells on the roof supply power, a NASA-developed aerogel insulates the interiors, and energy-saving pumps are used for wastewater, heating, cooling, circulation and drinking water. Water-powered heating converts the surrounding seawater into a free, efficient and clean natural heat source while reducing emissions by 81% compared to conventional heating using natural gas or oil. Furthermore, the heat transfer rate from water is higher than using the ground as a heat source.

Models

01-02 / Front perspective

03 / Detail
04 / Side view
05 / Entrance

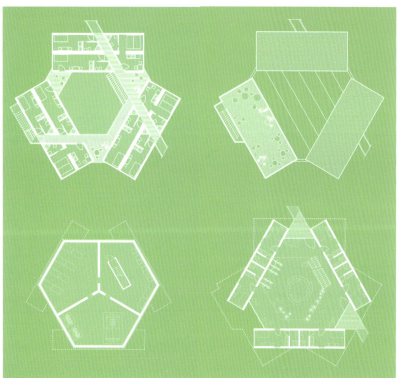

Site plans

06

05 / Room view
06 / Rest area by the river

Pocket House

Location Belo Horizonte, Minas Gerais, Brazil **Area** 504 square feet (47 square meters) **Completion date** 2013
Design Cristina Menezes **Photography** Jomar Bragança **Client** Menezes Arquitetura

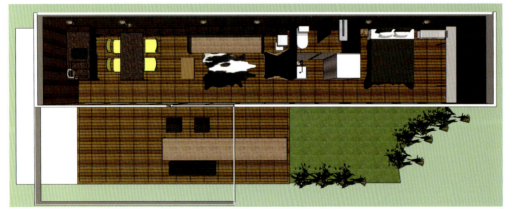

Top-down isometric sketch

The project, named Pocket House, was a home for a single man. The client wanted his home built out of a container in case he ever needed to move, he could easily transport his small house with him. He wanted the interior design to connect with nature. Consequently, the project's design revolved around the principles of mobility and sustainability.

Most of the construction work came down to building a support base for the container. Everything was just installation. The use of dry construction made the process go quickly and smoothly and allows the building to be transported with minimal difficulty in the future. Overall, the construction only took 10 days.

The used a single 40-foot (12-meter) long shipping container, measuring 4000 x 800 feet (1220 x 244 meters) externally. The total area of construction, however, including the deck outside of the container, amounted to 504 square feet (47 square meters). Nevertheless, to address the narrow space of the structure, the team cut the container's lateral steel walls to insert glass sliding doors. In this way, the interior smoothly integrated with the exterior. The large glass doors also help with natural ventilation and lighting.

All furniture used is easy to move around, allowing the client can use the deck as an extension of the living room and kitchen. The floor, walls, and ceiling were all coated with the same material: certified wood, making the space feel more expanisve. The glass bathroom walls bring more lighting and make the area feel less cramped. A translucent film applied onto the glass provides privacy between the living room and the bathroom.

For this project, the team successfully built a house with a kitchen, dining room, living room, bathroom and bedroom with just 323 square feet (30 square meters) of space inside the container. This project represents sustainability, a new and vital concept for living.

02

01 / Front side perspective
02-03 / Interior view

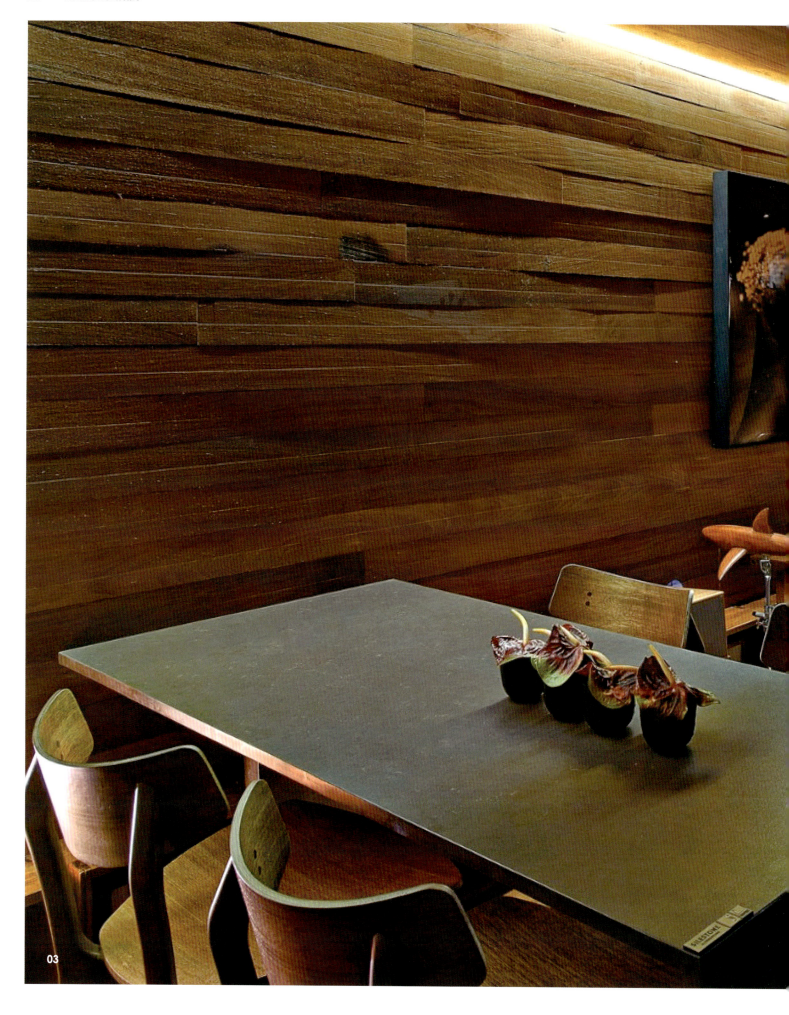

Un Dernier Voyage

Location Meuse, France **Area** 1184 square feet (110 square meters) **Completion date** 2014
Design Spray Architecture & Gabrielle Vella-Boucaud **Photography** Jelena Stajic

"Un Dernier Voyage" is a house project constructed on an old farmland, accessed by cutting through a forest path. The whole area rests on a hillside at the edge of a small village and a short distance away from the woodlands, which are filled with contemporary art pieces. Across the whole world, designers and artists come to this idyllic location. After much thought and consideration, after the client spent years of traveling overseas, "Un Dernier Voyage" is a coalescence of all the client's artistic influences.

The core idea in the design was to build a place of creation, a world where someone could seek inspiration. In one section, the structure is formed from a shipping container, altered to now function as a carving workshop. The structure is suspended with a slight incline by a metal apparatus. Six 20-meter containers are open wide to encourage a fluid circulation and a flexible interior layout. On the left and the right side of the bedroom and bathroom lie the living room and the office respectively, which are connected by a wide corridor where sculptures are exhibited. Two terraces are added to the structure. One is a covered entrance in the southwest and the other is an outdoor space in the northeast covered by a canopy spanning lengthwise with the house.

Elevation

According to brutalism principles, beautiful architecture is rooted in its economy. That is why the ceiling lays bare its metal structure, its steel sheeting, and technical equipment embedded there. Likewise, the floor is simply raw concrete. The black metal siding outside references the steel sheeting of a container. This black monolith contrasts with the rural landscape.However, if you stand on the hill overlooking the house, the long low shape of the black monolith perfectly blends into the green background. The facades are vertically drilled, either with French window openings, such as along the terrace, or with fixed windows that framed the landscape and played with the central axis of the structure. With the container workshop installed and oriented according to house, the house seems to be doubled in size.

"Un Dernier voyage" is raw housing in a wild landscape that echoes the long travels made by the containers as well as the person who lives in them.

01/ Entrance with covered terrace
02/ Terrace with sculptures
03/ House on stilts

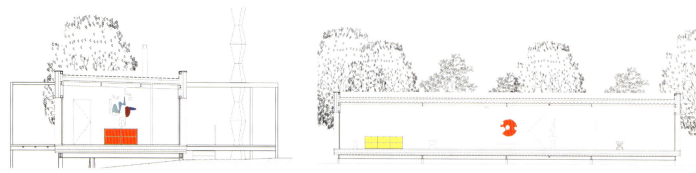

sectional

04 / Side view of terrace
05 / Garden next to terraces
06 / Living room

06

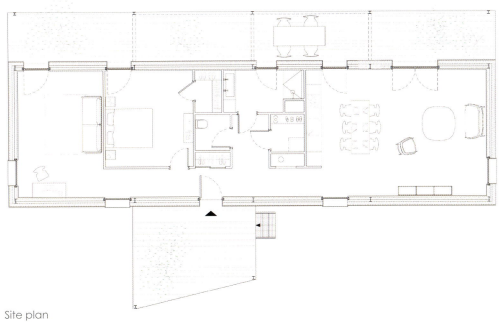

Site plan

07

07 / Office
08 / Bedroom

Cliff House

Location Johannesburg, South Africa **Area** 2260 square feet (210 square meters) **Completion date** 2017
Design Architecture for a change (pty) ltd **Photography** Architecture for a change (pty) ltd **Client** Mary Driscoll

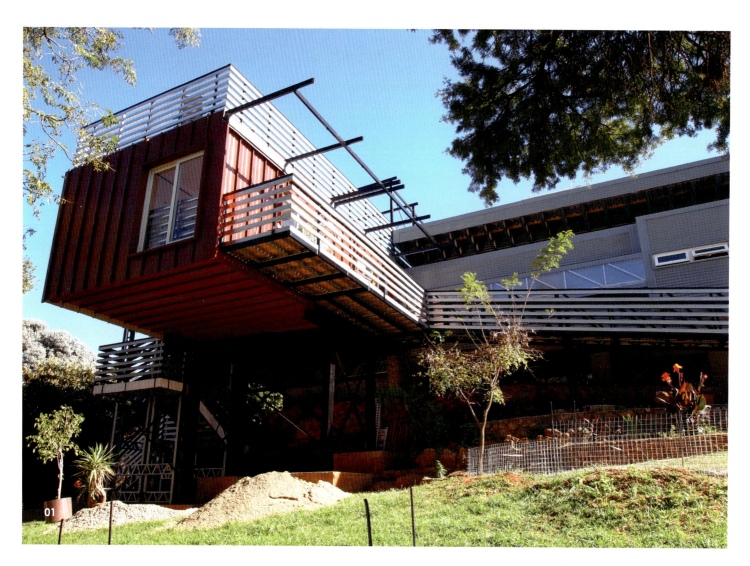

The central concept was to build a lightweight home that could function completely off the grid. Moreover, we wanted to adapt contemporary architectural theory to the local landscape. Sustainable architecture in South Africa is expensive and mostly unfeasible. Given our limited budget, we saw this project as an opportunity to push the boundaries of what is possible in sustainability and affordability, an important challenge in regards to the global economic state

We used lightweight construction methods both minimize the need for a concrete foundation and to reduce the environmental impact on the site. (The site overlooking an extreme drop was another factor in lightweight materials) We therefore incorporated two used shipping containers as structural cantilever elements. Although the containers were no longer suitable for shipping, they still worked excellently for up-cycling into structurally sound building blocks. The other half of the house was constructed from lightweight steel framing, pre-fabricated off-site. These frames were delivered to site inside the two containers. This gave the containers a second use as a logistical element within the building process.

01 / Container house cantilevered over the site
02 / Lightweight steel staircase

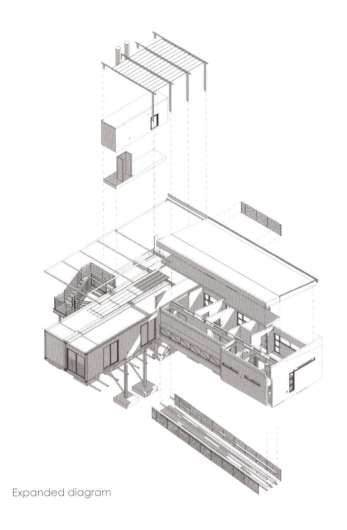

Expanded diagram

02

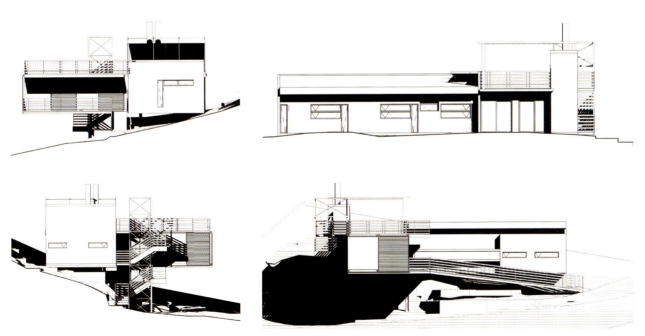

Side section

03

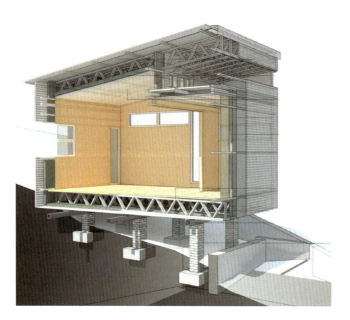

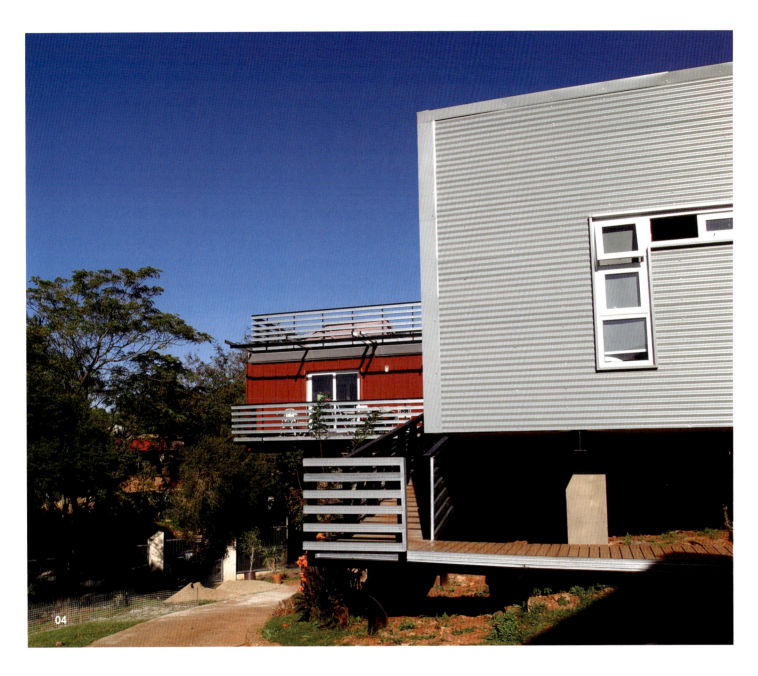

The composite walls inside consist of various layers, providing much more effective insulation than conventional brick and mortar structures used in South Africa. As another example of up-cycling, the insulation used was manufactured from waste plastic bottles. The floor finish itself is up-cycled, manufactured from discard cork.

The site is equipped with a borehole that pumps water onto the site, eliminating the need for a municipal water connection. Moreover, the house runs entirely off of solar power. Storing natural gas on site also allow cooking without connecting to a gas line.

In efforts to reduce the energy demands as much as possible, we designed the layout to optimize natural lighting as well as natural ventilation. Also, the window system used is a uPVC frame with double glazing to improve insulation level and avoid heat gains.

03 / Steel ramp
04 / Eastern facade

05

05 / Underside of house
06 / Interior design
07 / Roof deck

Nemo House

Location Youngam, South Korea **Completion date** 2013 **Design** Kangsoo Lee, Joohyung Kang, Taekho Lee, Yeongcheol Choi **Photography** Kangsoo Lee

01

The Nemo House was designed for a family looking for a new home in a typical rural area in South Korea surrounded by farmlands and mountains. At the same time, the project aimed to function as an alternative solution for economical housing. The Nemo House design consists of three shipping containers. Recycling empty containers for houses is one of the ways to create modern and inexpensive homes today worldwide. Also, the container's durability and water-resistance works well for adapting containers into a living shelter. However, the process of adaptation for permanent accomodations is challenging. Despite the numerous advantages, container housing in South Korea is mostly unprecedented and many examples that already exist are of poor quality. The Nemo House may be the first high-quality accommodation made of freight containers in South Korea.

For this reason, the Nemo House was exhibited to the public at Kyounghyang Housing Fair in 2013 before installed on site.. The exhibition provided good opportunity to show people a viable alternative in green living. The building showcased its portability and flexibility by being disassembled and reassembled in a short period of time. Container houses are affordable, sustainable and eco-friendly. It also blends recycled materials with creative ideas to reuse and recycle, turning useless or outdated empty containers into house that are efficient, functional and comfortable.

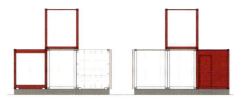

Cross-sectional sketch

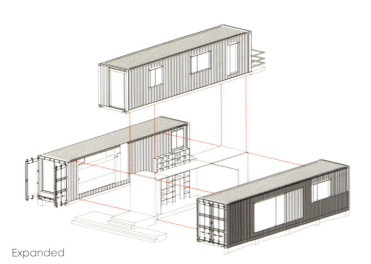

Expanded

'Nemo' in Korean refers to rectangular geometry. As the name of the house indicates, the project consists of a stacking together three freight containers, forming a two-story living space and a yard. The two 40-foot (12-meter) long containers, with a ceiling one foot (0.3 meters) higher than most containers, sit on the foundation facing each other with an 8-foot (2.4-meter) gap in between. This formation enables both the living room and kitchen to have larger width yet the gap is covered by the container sticking out on the second floor. The house is surrounded by green and lush vegetation, creating a pleasant and peaceful landscape, perfect for someone yearning for life in the country.

The building was designed to conserve more energy than it consumes by using up-cycled shipping containers as a steel structural frame, a sustainable wood cladding façade for the south facing, and permeable paving. The main floor offers a living room space made up of a kitchen with a dining area and stairs. In addition, the main floor holds a master bedroom, bathroom, and a laundry room. White decorations and a large see–through bookshelf reaching upstairs unites the living room, dining room, and kitchen into one open family space linked to the terrace deck. The second floor is configured to allow three equal-size playrooms for the family's two children, a hall with wooden bookshelf rising from downstairs, and a bedroom with big windows.

01 / Front perspective
02 / Side view
03 / Detail

The two bottom containers and the top container are staggered to create a projection to use as a porch and balcony. This strategy of staggering helps connects to the natural environment at the front and back door.

The south-facing façade employs large windows and wood cladding to hide some scratches on used container's corrugated steel surface and to complement its metal material. Limited budget made the design focus on improving thermal performance and heating system for harsh winter climate.

One of the great features of freight containers is utilizing the doors as a design factor. When the doors in dining area are open, the interior space can be expanded into patio. Furthermore, usage of the doors references back to the identity of the containers themselves. The Nemo House design is a functional, eco-friendly, inexpensive building with simple installation, requiring minimal effort and time. The designer hopes this project will help increase the popularity of small house designs made of empty shipping containers.

04

04-05 / Staircase
06 / Detail

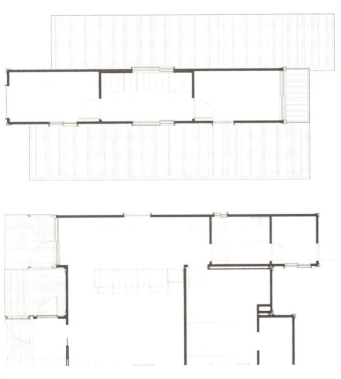

Floor plans

Studio for Two

Location New Delhi, India **Area** 1200 square feet (111 square meters) **Completion date** 2016
Design Studio Wood, Sahej Bhatia, Navya Aggarwal, Vrinda Mathur **Photography** Rohan Dayal
Client Rohit & Richa Aggarwal

Studio Wood was given a unique brief: designing a lightweight temporary accommodation on top of an apartment approximately 1200 square feet (111 square meters). The team was restricted by a tight deadline and by weight limitations. After a number of day spent brainstorming, the designers decided using metal girders and trusses to form the exoskeleton and thin steel panels refurbished from used shipping containers to wrap around the envelope.

A grid of 5 x 5 foot (1.5 x 1.5 meter) horizontal and vertical beams was laid out on the terrace floor to raise the floor height. The purpose of this was twofold. First, raising the floor height gives the room a floating feeling. Second, this avoids rainwater leaking into the structure.

The outer walls took support structure was built on the terrace, the ceiling plane was exploited as much as possible for daylight and natural ventilation with the addition of two skylights varying in width.

Having young entrepreneurs as the clients, the aim was to bridge the gap between work and play by designing a multi-purpose work studio by day and entertainment hub by night.

The space was divided into three zones: open outdoor area, the semi-open portico characterized by the wooden decking, and the closed cabin.

The entry to the cabin was marked by a three-part sliding UPVC glass door, allowing for a seamless integration of the interior space with the exterior. The semi-open cantilevered deck clad with wood gives the space a cozy feeling, making it the perfect place to enjoy a cup of tea in the morning.

The landscape is riddled with several playful features, including a swing and multipurpose cubes installed at varying heights. These structures could be moved around freely to create a new look each time.

Perhaps one of the most challenging features of this project was designing the sliding door for the outdoor bathroom. The 10-foot (3-meter) high door had to be designed to slide smoothly despite its heavy weight. This feat, however, was accomplished by using the ball bearing mechanisms predominantly used by automobile manufacturers, ensuring the door open and closed easily and with no issue.

04

01 / Exterior of studio
02 / Semi-open cantilevered deck
03 / Bathroom metal door
04 / Landscaping

Another prominent feature of the site was the multi-level feature wall. The design team constructed steel ladder-like elements and placed custom-made fiberboard planters on the ladders at different levels. With this technique, the greenery was not only the part of the floor but also encompassed the entire wall.

The interior was designed to echo the concept of flexibility. With a simple push, the sofa can transform into a bed while still able to comfortably sit five people.

This design was born with climate also at the forefront. Special care in landscaping with plants was done to create a microclimate to mitigate heat.

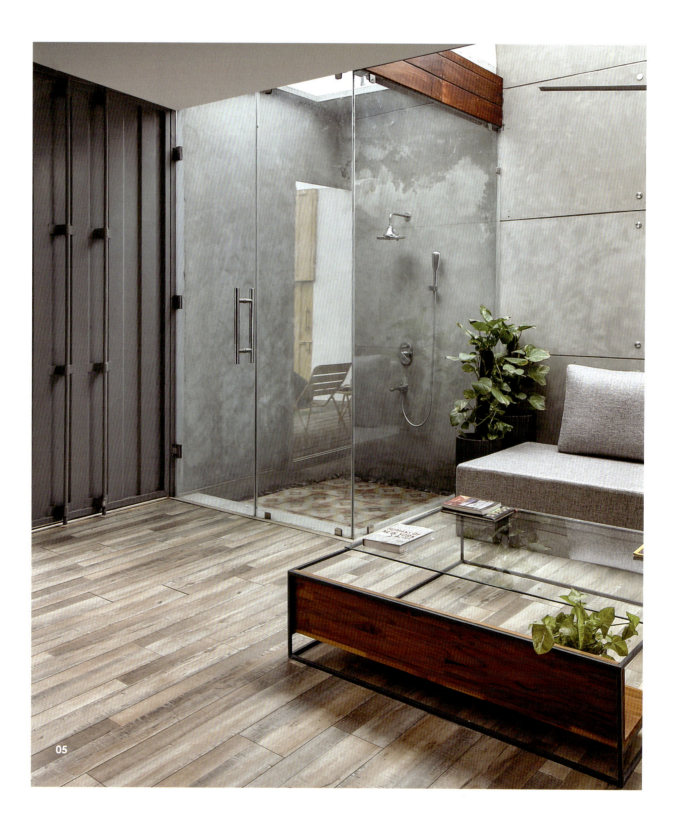

05

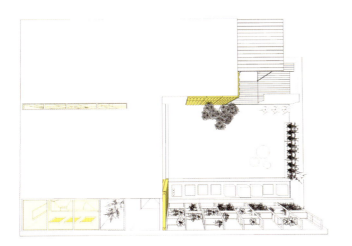

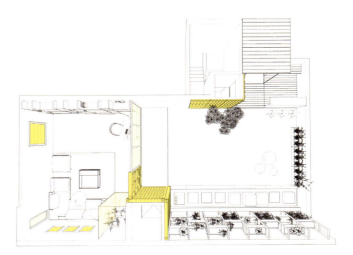

Roof Plan

Floor Plan

05 / Open-air bathing area
06 / Studio interior

06

UNIONKUL STACK II

Location Copenhagen, Denmark. **Area** 10,764 square feet (1000 square meters) **Completion date** 2016
Design Arcgency **Photography** COAST_ Arcgency **Client** UNIONKUL A/S

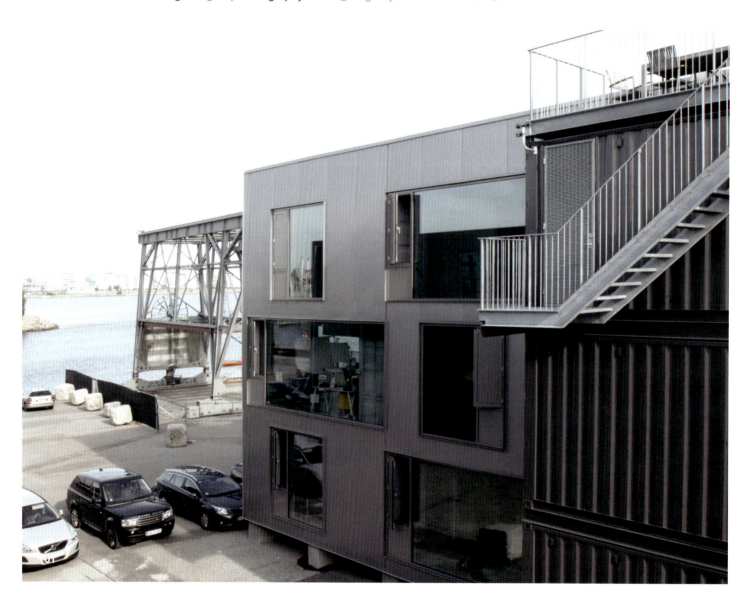

Specifically designed for sites in transition, STACK II aims to offer excellent working conditions within a limited time frame. When the time comes for the land to be developed, the building is designed to be disassembled and either moved to a new temporary location or reused as components in a new building.

The design builds on the same principles as STACK I, but has been further developed in collaboration with a visionary client based on know-how gathered from the first project. STACK II is a product and a model for a temporary office that is fast to build, sustainable, and feasible. The structure is placed right besides STACK I and together they overlook the harbour, creating a vibrant framework for creative businesses and start-ups.

The key sustainable features of STACK II include: adapted for Scandinavian climate (temperatures range from – 10 to 25 degrees Celsius), energy usage below 12.5 kWh/square foot (41 kWh/square meter) per year, highly insulated facade panels(300mm. U- value: 0.13 W/m2K), made out of 90 % recyclable materials, naturally ventilated, 3-layered windows covered with a shading film, and constructed pillars with minimal impact to site.

The entire load-bearing structure of STACK II consists of 20-foot high freight containers. They are aligned in two rows and stacked three stories high in a checkered formation. The gap between the containers can be modified to suit different needs. The gap can be left open or floor elements can be inserted. This offers a high level of flexibility in use, as the building can adapt to a fluctuating number of occupants.

01 / Facade clad in insulation panels

02 / Broad windows giving excellent natural light in office

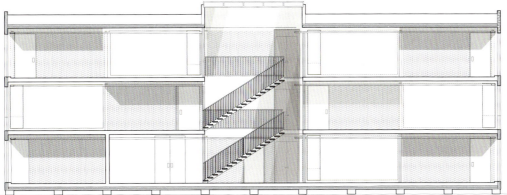

Cross-section

03

The building itself is suspended off the ground on pillars. High-performance insulation sandwich panels wrap around all six sides of the building. This creates an airtight shell, crucial to minimizing heat loss. The use of pillars as opposed to a traditional foundation causes a minimal impact on the site and makes the building moveable. STACK II shows a very pragmatic attitude towards container aesthetics. Due to the need for insulation, the containers are covered on the outside, but visible on the interior and through openings in the facade. This creates a distinct separation between inside and outside. Placed left of the entrance stands a tower of exposed containers. The tower has a practical function as fire escape, but works also figuratively to show the nature of the building and to mark the entrance. All technical installations are visible. They become part of the architectural expression and at the same time, remain easy to access and disassemble.

The large windows let the light penetrate the building and provide generous views over the waterfront and harbour. Their size and position emphasizes the checkered system of the stacked containers. Interior windows enable visual exchange between the individual workspaces, but allow each room to still feel private. This, along with the shared communal spaces, creates a good working environment and a collaborative atmosphere.

03 / Exposed container next to rest of structure

04 / Communal space

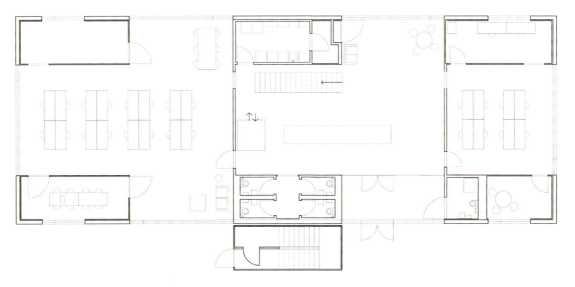

First-floor plan.

Stack II is expected to be in use in Nordhavnen for only 10-12 years. It had to be built quickly, cheaply, and sustainably for the construction and later removal of the building. That is why the structure was built using a modular principle and only a few materials. This makes it possible to disassemble the entire building and move it, or parts of it, to another location or to reuse the materials in a new building.

With the continuous decline of industry in the cities and a growing sector of smaller companies, start-ups and creative, there is a demand for buildings that can exploit otherwise derelict land and provide affordable work space. STACK II is a model to fulfill both these needs in a way that is sustainable and financially feasible.

05 / Industrial central staircase

06 / Floor space spanning two containers

07 / Open office area

CONTAINER SALE OFFICE

Location Shanghai, China **Area** 2906 square feet (270 square meters) **Completion date** 2016
Design Atelier XÜK **Photography** Shengliang SU

01

Located in the Qingpu district of Shanghai, the project put together a sales office for a commercial complex right near it. The office is a temporary construction that will later be dismantled when the surrounding urban area has been fully developed. Given the situation, the client wanted to use shipping containers as the primary building element due to the added efficiency and speed in construction.

The design process then approached the project with one practical issue: how to maximize the building space with the minimum number of containers? The answer the team came up with was a basic offset-piling strategy. Such a method saved a large number of containers and formed a double-height atrium well suited for display purposes.

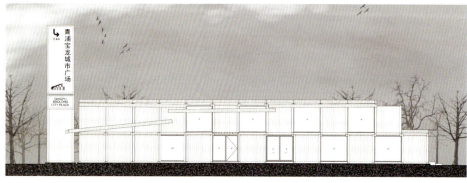

Cross-sectional sketch

The atrium is symmetrically aligned with the main entrance. Its simple but strong presence accentuates the interior and exterior of the building. The lighting system was designed with the space in mind. Customized wall washers were installed to light up the staggered walls, creating an interesting shift between day and night. In the daytime, openings on the wall provide illumination to the atrium. At night, light reflected off of the solid walls does the same job.

The administrative space for the building, such as meeting rooms and office, are at the end of the atrium. A wooden staircase was designed to take people up to a small meeting room on the second floor with a view overlooking the atrium. The administrative space was efficiently designed in terms of space. All HVAC utilities were installed in the partition walls instead of the ceiling to increase vertical space.

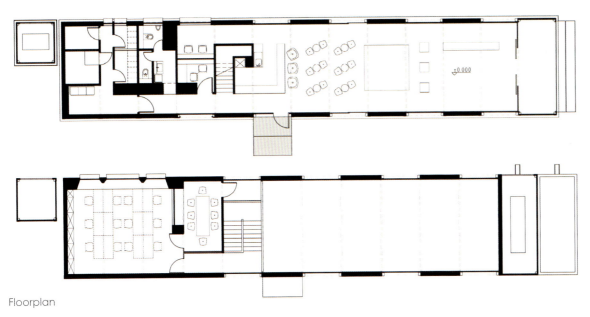

Floorplan

01/Side perspective
02/Entrance

04

04 / Detail
05 / Staircase
06 / Second floor

Bee+

Location South Software Park, Zhuhai, Guangdong Province, China **Area** 15069 square feet (1400 square meters)
Completion date 2016 **Design** Studio Cullinan and Buck Architects Ltd.
Photography Studio Cullinan and Buck Architects Ltd.

Located in the south of China, Bee+ Co-Working Space in Zhuhai was the first project of Bee+. It was constructed with 36 containers and steel frames. The building includes a co-working space, a restaurant, and a roof garden bar. Bee+ Zhuhai was designed by an non-architectural designer. In 2015, the team came up with an idea of constructing a co-working space using containers. After consulting with some architectural design companies, the team simply decided to design this building themselves, due to the expensive design fees. In the beginning, the team did not actually have a clearly concept what the building would look like and all they knew was that the result had to be cool The team used a style akin to Lego blocks to construct the general shape, while planning different functional areas inside the containers. When the initial shape had been drawn, the team used SketchUp to build a model, and then sent this model to a professional architecture design firm who helped adjust the designs to look more professional.

01-02 / Side view

03 / Aerial view
04 / Staircase

05 / Bar
06-07 / Interior view
08 / Kitchen
09 / Fitness club

Tidal Container Office

Location Beijing, China **Area** 1615 square feet (150 square meters) **Completion date** 2015
Design Ke Chang, Wenhan LI **Photography** Haiting Sun, Ke Chang

The tide is a natural phenomenon in coastal areas. The tide is the periodic fluctuation in the movement of seawater caused by the moon's gravitational force. Tides are a kind of social phenomenon in contemporary China. The annual travel rush during Spring Festival being one example, people frequently move around due the huge difference in opportunities between city and country life. Because of high housing prices, more and more young people have to live on the outskirts of the city. They live a tidal life, flowing back and forth between home and work.

The cause of this 'tidal' phenomenon is improperly utilized urban space. Underutilized space simply becomes a waste of social value. Given the situation, is it possible to compress this citywide tidal flow into a narrow concrete space? Sketching out a time of what would be needed when, the functions of home, office, and public space collapse into one design.

A new office is a chaotic environment. The organization for every project is tentative and always subject to change. During this stage, the office layout is uncertain. Different frameworks are being generated every day. A normal space cannot fulfill the demands of a rapidly changing startup.

As a design office, the project needed not only a working space, but also an auxiliary space for relaxation, recreation, eating, design modeling, and conducting meetings With an area of only 861 square feet (80 square meters), how could we combine these functions into one place? The Tidal Container Office makes this happen.

02

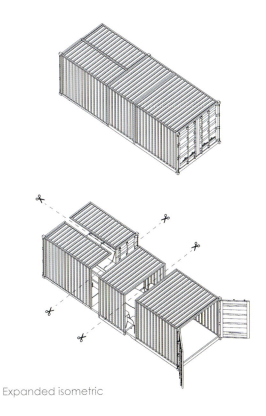

Expanded isometric

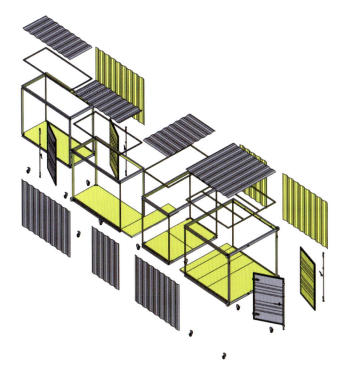

03-05 / Functional spaces of container
06 / Tidal Container Office

06

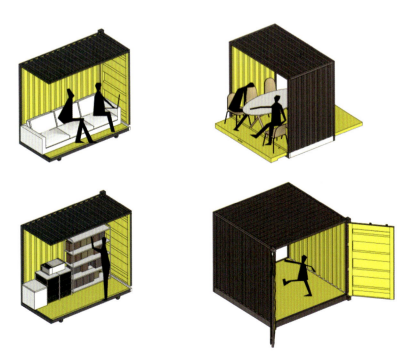

Diagram of functions

Innovation Studios

Location Rochester, United Kingdom **Area** 9688 square feet (900 square meters) **Completion date** 2017
Developer QED Sustainable Urban Developments **Design** Cityzen **Photography** Formatt Design & Photography

Innovation Studios Strood is a purpose-built development of 15 office spaces and 18 storage units that has been created using a kit of moveable and reusable parts based on re-purposed shipping containers, offering a sustainable, robust, and affordable solution to the high demand for enterprise space.

The development, located the previously derelict bank of the River Medway, is part of the Medway Council's ambitious 20-year program to regenerate the waterfront and make Watermill Wharf a hub for entrepreneurs.

Solar (PV) panels on the roof will provide some of the required power for the development with any additional power fed back into the grid. All units feature a kitchen, toilet facilities, a bookable meeting room, and a secure bicycle storage area.

The development specifically targets creative digital and technology start-ups and burgeoning micro-firms. Companies based at Innovation Studios Strood will benefit from the business support services provided by the nearby Innovation Centre Medway (ICM), such as exceptional broadband quality, meeting rooms, networking events and training opportunities.

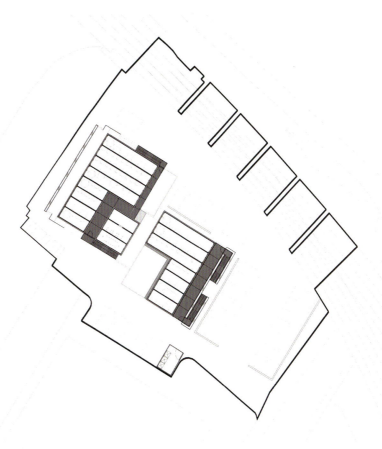

Site plan (not to scale)

01 / South elevation of Block A viewed from car park
02 / North elevation of Block B viewed from across the River Medway
03 / Stairway to office units in Block A

04

05

04 / South elevation of Block C including communal kitchen unit, bathroom and board room
05 / Side view of Block B with cedral board cladding
06 / Storage units underneath Block B offices
07 / Internal walkway servicing first-floor office units and connecting Block B and C

Joshua Tree

Location Joshua Tree, California, U.S.A **Area** 2153 square feet (200 square meters) **Completion date** 2017
Design Whitaker Studio **Photography** Whitaker Studio

01

This design started in 2010 when an advertising agency approached the designer to design them an office for their new company. By the time that we started talking, they had already been thinking about using shipping containers and so the designer started to explore what they could do with them as a basic building block. The local architecture is predominately low rise, with a few historical buildings peppered the landscape, such as Hohenzollern Castle. As a new advertising agency, they needed a building that stood out. So, thinking about Hohenzollern Castle and drawing inspiration from crystal growth in laboratories, the design evolved into a semi-circle of containers radiating out from a central meeting space, creating office bays at ground level and skylights above. Sadly, the advertising agency stopped before it started and the office was never built.

However, as the design was never anchored to a specific location, the designer was always keen to find a new life for it elsewhere. In 2017, a client approached the designer to develop the design as a private residence for their site in Joshua Tree, California. As soon as the designer saw the landscape of their site, scattered with jagged rocks, it felt like the natural home for the concept. The plan pairs containers together to form V-shaped en-suite bedrooms. These array around the cluster of containers to form the main living and dining space, with additional containers forming the entrance and utility spaces. When arranging the plan, each space was orientated to either frame a specific view or to use the topography of the site for privacy. The containers that point skyward are placed carefully within the composition, sometimes to lower a wall between adjacent ground floor containers, connecting the spaces together; at other times their purpose is to bring light deep into the plan.

01 / Joshua Tree exterior
02 / Bedroom
03 / Kitchen

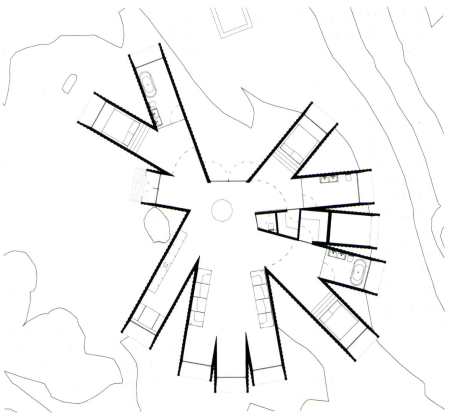

Site plan

04

04 / Living room and kitchen
05 / Bedroom and ensuite bathroom

05

Index

Devil's Corner
Cumulus Studio
Web:https://cumulus.studio/
Tel:03 6231 4841
Email:peter@cumulus.studio

Zhao Hua Xi Shi Living Museum
IAPA Design Consultants
Web:http://www.iapa.net.au/
Tel: 86-20-38259596
Email Info@iapa.net.au

APAP OPEN SCHOOL
LOTEK, Ada Tolla + Giuseppe Lignano, Principals,
Tommy Manuel, Project

Seoul youth zone
Kangsoo Lee, Joohyung Kang, Jinyoung
Oh,Taekho Lee
Web:http://www.thinktr.com/
Tel: + 82 (0)2 6487 3338
Email: klee.think@gmail.com

OceanScope
AnL Studio (Keehyun Ahn and Minsoo
Lee), ZZangPD (Chang Gil-Hwang)
Architecture+Interior Designers

Jazzboksen 2016
mmw arkitekter as one
Web:http://www.mmw.no/
Tel:+47 22 17 34 40
Email:mail@mmw.no

Conteneur Bell
Hatem+D
Web:http://hatem.ca/
Tel:418 524-1554
Email: info@hatem.ca

Dunraven Container Sports Hall
Studio Cullinan And Buck Architects Ltd.
Web:www.scabal.net
Tel:+44 (0) 20 7033 8788
Email:Dominic.Cullinan@scabal.net

KontenerART 2012
mode:lina
Web:http://www.modelina-architekci.com/
Tel: +48 61 223 12 12
Email:HELLO@MODELINA-ARCHITEKCI.COM

Hai d3
ibda design
Web:http://ibdadesign.com/
Tel:00971 4 2055 300

Taitung Aboriginal Galleria
Bio-Architecture Formosana
Web:http://www.bioarch.com.tw/
Tel:+886 2 25923535
Email:arch@bioarch.com.tw

Nomadic Museum
Shigeru Ban Architects
Web:http://www.shigerubanarchitects.com/
Tel:Tokyo Office: +81-(0)3-3324-6760
Paris Office: +33 (0)1 70 71 20 50
America Office: +1 212 925 2211
Email:tokyo@shigerubanarchitects.com(Tokyo office)
europe@shigerubanarchitects.com(Paris office)
America@shigerubanarchitects.com(USA office)

Marche in the forest
Hiroaki Kajiura Environment Architecture Design
Office Hiroaki Kajiura
Web:http://kajiura-a.com
Tel:0586-86-8436
Email:kajiura-architect@fine.ocn.ne.jp

So Table Kobe0330
A.S.A.P.designlab,Katsuyoshi Shindoh,DALIAN
GEKEA MODULAR THECHNOLOGY Co.,LTD
Web:http://www.asapdesignlab.com/
Tel:090-3970-0500

ContainHotel
ARTIKUL architects - Ing. arch. Pavel Lejdar, Ing. arch. Jan Gabriel, Ing. arch. Jakub Vlcek
Web:WWW.ARTIKUL.EU
Tel:+420 603 546 909
Email: HONZA@ARTIKUL.EU

Ccasa Hostel
Ngo Tuan Anh

Alphaville Store
contain[it]+SuperLimão Studio
Web:www.superlimao.com.br
www.contanit.com.br
Tel:+55 11 3518 8919
Email:livia@rpnacobogo.com.br

CRE-Box
Shanghai Kefan Investment Co.,Ltd.
http://www.kefan.com/index.php
+86 21 6428 7165
jinye@kefan.com

Pop Brixton
Carl Turner Architects
Web:http://www.ct-architects.co.uk/

THE KRANE
Arcgency
Web:http://arcgency.com/
Tel:+45 6128 0012
Email:moller@arcgency.com

MaxHaus Paulista
GTM Cenografia
Web:www.gtmcenografia.com.br
Tel:+55 11 3024-4400
Email:andrea.miyata@gtmcenografia.com.br

Bonaire Street Market
MESURA Partners in Architecture & vdv /
Web:www.mesura.eu
Tel:+34 934672190
Email:admin@mesura.eu

Container Stack Pavilion
People's Architecture Office(He Zhe, James Shen, Zang Feng)
Web:http://www.peoples-architecture.com & http://www.peoples-products.com
Email:office@peoples-architecture.com

Vehicle Charging Station
STAXBOND Buildings Technology Company Limited.
Tel: +86 757 2897 6870
Email: koeyhe@staxbond.com

Estoril Praia Clube
Ilona Galant, Yaroslav Galant
Web:http://yaroslavgalant.com/raboty/
Tel: +38 (097) 878 53 41
Email:ilona@yaroslavgalant.com

Wisdom Bay
Shanghai Kefan Investment Co.,Ltd.
Web:http://www.kefan.com/index.php
Tel:+86 21 6428 7165
Email:jinye@kefan.com

UNIT Cafe
TSEH Architectural Group
Web:tseh.com.ua
Tel:+3 8 044 2270545
Email: info@tseh.com.ua

Nike Unlimited Rio
GTM Cenografia
Web:www.gtmcenografia.com.br
Tel:+55 11 3024-4400
Email:andrea.miyata@gtmcenografia.com.br

HATAGOYA EBISU HOTEL
Atelier Mugi Architect Office/IDMobile co.,LTD
Atelier Mugi Architect Office/IDMobile co.,LTD
Web:https://atelier-mugi.jimdo.com
Tel:+81-6-7502-4790

Zhengda Colorful City Container Residence Design
Shanghai HuaDu Architecture and Urban Design Group (HDD) Haiao Zhang
Web:http://hdd-group.com/zw/index.php
Tel:86-21-65975399
Email:hdd@hdd-gtoup.com

Plugin Tower
People's Architecture Office(He Zhe, James Shen, Zang Feng)
Web:http://www.peoples-architecture.com & http://www.peoples-products.com
Email:office@peoples-architecture.com

Container Casulo
Bernardo Horta Arquiteto, MEIUS Arquitetura, Aerolito Arquitetura
Web:http://meius.com.br/
Tel:55 (31) 2552-0107

Urban Rigger
BIG-Bjarke Ingels Group
Web:http://www.big.dk/
Tel: +45.7221.7227
Email: big@big.dk

Un Dernier voyage
Spray Architecture & Gabrielle Vella-Boucaud
Web:http://sprayarchitecture.tumblr.com/
Tel:+33(0)7 86 26 88 59
Email:contact@sprayarchitecture.com

Nemo House
Kangsoo Lee, Joohyung Kang, Taekho Lee,Yeongcheol Choi
Web:http://www.thinktr.com/
Tel: + 82 (0)2 6487 3338
Email: klee.think@gmail.com

UNIONKUL STACK II
Arcgency
Web:http://arcgency.com/
Tel:+45 6128 0012
Email:moller@arcgency.com

Bee+
Studio Cullinan and Buck Architects Ltd.
Web:www.scabal.net
Tel:+44 (0) 20 7033 8788
Email:Dominic.Cullinan@scabal.net

Innovation Studios
Cityzen
Web:http://cityzendesign.co.uk/
Tel:+44 (0)1273 704901

Módulos habitacionales temporales
Felipe Ehrenfeld L.,Ignacio Orfali H., Ignacio Prieto I.
Web:http://labarq.cl/

The WFH House
Arcgency
Web:http://arcgency.com/
Tel:+45 6128 0012
Email:moller@arcgency.com

Pocket House
Cristina Menezes
Web:http://www.cristinamenezes.com.br/site/br/
Tel:55 31 999520309
Email:cristina@cristinamenezes.com.br

Cliff house
Architecture for a change (pty) ltd
Web:https://www.a4ac.co.za/

Studio for Two
Studio Wood, Sahej Bhatia, Navya Aggarwal, Vrinda Mathur
Web:http://studiowood.co.in/
Tel:+91 98-106-31311
Email:hello@studiowood.co.in

CONTAINER SALE OFFICE
Atelier XÜK
Web:http://www.atelier-xuk.com.cn/

TIDAL CON-TAINER OFFICE
Ke Chang, Wenhan LI
Web:http://www.officeproject.cn/
Tel:86 15011510733
Email:contact@officeproject.cn

Joshua Tree
Whitaker Studio
Web:http://www.whitakerstudio.co.uk/
Tel:+447717330910
Email: enquiries@whitakerstudio.co.uk

Published in Australia in 2018 by
The Images Publishing Group Pty Ltd
Shanghai Office
ABN 89 059 734 431
6 Bastow Place, Mulgrave, Victoria 3170, Australia
Tel: +61 3 9561 5544 Fax: +61 3 9561 4860
books@imagespublishing.com
www.imagespublishing.com

Copyright © The Images Publishing Group Pty Ltd 2018
The Images Publishing Group Reference Number: 1452

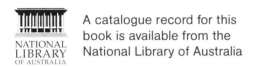

A catalogue record for this
book is available from the
National Library of Australia

Title: Movable Architecture
Author: Edited by Ross Gilbert
ISBN: 9781864707694

Production manager | Group art director: Nicole Boehringer
Senior editor: Gina Tsarouhas
Assisting editor: Benjamin Sepsenwol

Printed by Everbest Printing Investment Limited, in Hong Kong/China

IMAGES has included on its website a page for special notices in relation to this and its other
publications. Please visit www.imagespublishing.com